THE GLORIOUS HISTORY OF REDEMPTION

A Compact Survey
Of the Old and New Testaments

James O. Boyd

&

J. Gresham Machen

SOLID GROUND CHRISTIAN BOOKS
BIRMINGHAM, ALABAMA USA

Solid Ground Christian Books
PO Box 660132
Vestavia Hills AL 35266
205-443-0311
mike.sgcb@gmail.com
www.solid-ground-books.com

The Glorious History of Redemption
A Compact Survey of the Old and New Testaments
James Oscar Boyd (1874-1947)
John Gresham Machen (1881-1937)

Originally published in 1922 by The Westminster Press
Entitled "A Brief Bible History: A Survey of the Old
and New Testaments"

First Solid Ground Edition – June 2013

Cover design by Borgo Design
Contact them at borgogirl@bellsouth.net

ISBN- 978-159925-289-6

Contents

Section I

THE DEVELOPMENT OF THE CHURCH IN OLD TESTAMENT TIMES

Section II

THE LIFE OF CHRIST AND THE DEVELOPMENT OF THE CHURCH IN NEW TESTAMENT TIMES

CONTENTS

Introduction

This book surveys the history of God's redeeming grace. It reviews Old Testament history, disclosing the stream of God's redeeming purposes flowing down through the older times. It reviews New Testament history, disclosing the broadening and deepening of that purpose for us men and for mankind in our Lord and Saviour Jesus Christ and his Church.

The chapters included in this book appear also as a part of Teaching the Teacher, a First Book in Teacher Training, and are issued in this form to supply the demand for a brief Bible history, for popular reading.

HAROLD McA. ROBINSON.

SECTION I

The Development of the Church in Old Testament Times

By James Oscar Boyd, Ph.D., D.D.

LESSON I

Before Abraham

Genesis, Chapters 1 to 11

That part of the globe which comes within the view of the Old Testament is mostly the region, about fifteen hundred miles square, lying in the southwestern part of Asia, the southeastern part of Europe, and the northeastern part of Africa. This is where the three continents of the Eastern Hemisphere come together. Roughly speaking it includes Asia Minor, Mesopotamia, Syria, Palestine, Arabia, and Egypt, with a fringe of other lands and islands stretching beyond them.

The heart of all this territory is that little strip of land, lying between the desert on the east and the Mediterranean Sea on the west, known as Syria and Palestine. It is some four hundred miles in length and varies from fifty to one hundred miles in width. It has been well called "the bridge of the world," for like a bridge it joins the largest continent, Asia, to the next largest, Africa. And as Palestine binds the lands together, so the famous Suez Canal at its southern end now binds the seas together. To-day, therefore, as in all the past, this spot is the crossroads of the nations.

Palestine has long been called the "Holy Land," because it is the scene of most of the Bible story. Yet it would be a mistake to suppose that that Bible story is limited to Palestine. The book of Genesis does not introduce the reader to Canaan (as it calls Palestine) until he has reached its twelfth chapter. There is a sense in which the history of God's people begins with Abraham, and it was Abraham who went at God's bidding into the land of Canaan. The story of Abraham will be taken up in the second lesson; but the Bible puts before the life of Abraham all the familiar story that lies in the first eleven chapters of Genesis and that forms the background for the figures of Abraham and his descendants.

The location of this background is the basin of the Tigris and Euphrates Rivers. These two streams are mentioned in Gen. 2 : 14 (the Tigris under the form "Hiddekel") as the third and fourth "heads"

7

of the "river that went out of Eden to water the garden" in which our first parents dwelt. The region is at the southern end of what is now called Mesopotamia. At the northern end of this river basin towers the superb mountain known as Mount Ararat. But the "mountains of Ararat," mentioned in Gen. 8 : 4 as the place where Noah's ark rested when the waters of the Flood had subsided, are no particular peak, but are the highlands of Kurdistan, which in ancient times were called Urartu (Ararat). Between Kurdistan on the north and the Persian Gulf on the south, the highlands of Persia on the east and the great Syrian Desert on the west, occurred the earliest drama of human history.

That drama was a tragedy. It became a tragedy because of man's sin. The wonderful poem of creation in Gen., ch. 1, has for the refrain of its six stanzas, "God saw that it was good." Best of all was man, the last and highest of God's works—man, made in "his own image," after his likeness. On the sixth "day," when God made man, God said of his work, "Behold, it was very good." More than that: through the kindness of God man is put in a "garden," and is ordered to "dress it and to keep it." Ch. 2 : 15. Adam sees his superiority to the rest of the animal kingdom, over which he is given "dominion." He is thus prepared to appreciate the woman as a helpmeet for him, so that the unit of society may ever mean for him one man and one woman with their children. Adam is also warned against sin as having disobedience for its root and death as its result.

All this prepares us to understand the temptation, the miserable fall of the woman and the man, their terror, shame, and punishment. Ch. 3. And we are not surprised to see the unfolding of sin in the life of their descendants, beginning with Cain's murder of Abel, and growing until God sweeps all away in a universal deluge. Chs. 4, 6.

God's tender love for his foolish, rebellious creatures "will not let them go." At the gates of the garden from which their sin has forever banished them, God already declares his purpose to "bruise" the head of that serpent, Rom. 16 : 20, who had brought "sin into the world and death by sin," Gen. 3 : 15. Through the "seed of the woman"—a "Son of man" of some future day—sinful man can escape the death he has brought upon himself. And from Seth, the child "appointed instead of" murdered Abel, a line of men descends, who believe this promise of God. Ch. 5. In Enoch we find them "walking with God," v. 24, in a fellowship that seemed lost when paradise was lost. In Lamech we find them hoping with each new generation that God's curse will be at length removed. V. 29. And in Noah we find them obedient to a positive command of God, ch. 6 : 22, as Adam had been disobedient.

In the Flood, Noah and his family of eight were the only persons to survive. When they had come from the ark after the Flood, God gave them the promise that he would not again wipe out "all flesh." Ch. 9 : 11. But after it appeared that God's judgments had not made them fear him, God was just as angry with Noah's descendants as he had been with the men before the Flood. Pride led them to build a tower to be a rallying point for their worship of self. But God showed them that men cannot long work together with a sinful purpose as their common object; he broke up their unity in sin by confusing their speech, ch. 11, and scattering them over the earth, ch. 10. This second disappointment found its brighter side in the line of men descended from Noah through Shem, ch. 11 : 10, who also cherished God's promises. And the last stroke of the writer's pen in these earliest chapters of the Bible introduces the reader to the family of Terah in that line of Shem, and thus prepares the way for a closer acquaintance with Terah's son, Abraham, "the friend of God."

QUESTIONS ON LESSON I

1. About how large is the world of the Old Testament, and where does it lie?
2. What special importance has Palestine because of its position?
3. How much of the story in Genesis is told before we are carried to Palestine?
4. Locate on a map the scene of those earliest events in human history.
5. Show how the first two chapters of Genesis prepare for the tragedy of sin and death that follows.
6. How does the brighter side of hope and faith appear from Adam to Noah?
7. What effect did the Flood have on men's sin and their faith in God?
8. Trace the descent of the man God chose to become "the father of the faithful."

LESSON II
The Patriarchs

Genesis, Chapters 12 to 50

God's purpose to save and bless all mankind was to be carried out in a wonderful way. He selected and "called" one man to become the head and ancestor of a single nation. And in this man and the nation descended from him, God purposed to bless the whole world.

Abraham was that man, and Israel was that nation. God made known his purpose in what the Bible calls the Promise, Gal. 3 : 17, the Blessing, v. 14, or the Covenant, v. 17. Its terms are given many times over in the book of Genesis, but the essence of it lies already in the first word of God to Abraham, Gen. 12 : 3, "In thee shall all the families of the earth be blessed."

To believe this promise was a work of faith. It was against all appearances and all probability. Yet this was just where the religious value of that promise lay for Abraham and for his children after him —in faith. They had to believe something on the basis solely of their confidence in the One who had promised it. Or rather, they had to believe in that Person, the personal Jehovah, their God. They must absolutely trust him. To do so, they must "know him." And that they might know him, he must reveal himself to them. That is why we read all through Genesis of God's "appearing" or "speaking" to this or the other patriarch. However he accomplished it, God was always trying thus to make them better acquainted with himself; for such knowledge was to be the basis of their faith. Upon faith in him depended their faith in his word, and upon faith in his word depended their power to keep alive in the world that true religion which was destined for all men and which we to-day share. Abraham's God is our God.

Not Abraham's great wealth in servants, Gen. 14 : 14, and in flocks and herds, ch. 13 : 2, 6, but the promise of God to bless, constituted the true "birthright" in Abraham's family. Ishmael, the child of doubt, missed it; and Isaac, the child of faith, obtained it. Gal. 4 : 23. Esau "despised" it, because he was "a profane [irreligious] person," Heb. 12 : 16, and Jacob schemed to obtain it by purchase, Gen. 25 : 31, and by fraud, ch. 27 : 19. Jacob bequeathed it to his sons, ch. 49, and

Moses delivered it in memorable poetic form to the nation to retain and rehearse forever. Deut., ch. 32.

When Abraham, the son of Terah, entered Canaan with Sarah his wife and Lot his nephew and their great company of servants and followers, he was obeying the command of his God. He no sooner enters it than God gives him a promise that binds up this land with him and his descendants. Gen. 13 : 14–17. Yet we must not suppose that Abraham settled down in this Promised Land in the way that the Pilgrim Fathers settled in the Old Colony. Although Canaan is promised to the "seed" of Abraham, Isaac, and Jacob as a possession, they did not themselves obtain a foothold in it. Apart from the field of the cave Machpelah, at Hebron in the south, Gen., ch. 23, and a "shoulder" (*shechem*) or fragment of land near Shechem ("Jacob's Well"), in the center of Canaan, the patriarchs did not acquire a foot of the soil of what was to become "the Holy Land." Abraham wandered about, even going down to Egypt and back. Isaac was sometimes at Hebron and sometimes at Beer-sheba on the extreme southern verge of the land. Jacob spent much of his manhood in Mesopotamia, and of his old age in Egypt. For after divine Providence in a remarkable manner had transplanted one of Jacob's sons, Joseph, into new soil, Gen., ch. 37, his father and his brothers were drawn after him, with the way for their long Egyptian residence providentially prepared for them, Gen. 50 : 20.

Side by side with the growth of a nation out of an individual we find God's choice of the direction which that growth should take. Not all, even of Abraham's family, were to become part of the future people of God. So Lot, Abraham's nephew, separates from him, and thereafter he and his descendants, the Ammonites and the Moabites, go their own way. As between Abraham's sons, Ishmael is cast out, and Isaac, Sarah's son, is selected. And between Isaac's two sons, Esau and Jacob, the choice falls on Jacob. All twelve of Jacob's sons are included in the purpose of God, and for this reason the nation is called after Jacob, though usually under his name "Israel," which God gave him after his experience of wrestling with "the angel of the Lord" at the river Jabbok. Gen. 32 : 22. Those sons of his are to become the heads of the future nation of the "twelve tribes", Acts 26: 7.

Even while Lot, Ishmael, and Esau are thus being cut off, the greatest care is taken to keep the descent of the future nation pure to the blood of Terah's house. Those three men all married alien wives:

Lot probably a woman of Sodom, Ishmael an Egyptian, and Esau two Hittite women. The mother of Isaac was Sarah, the mother of Jacob was Rebekah, and the mothers of eight of the twelve sons of Jacob were Leah and Rachel; and all these women belonged to that same house of Terah to which their husbands belonged. Indeed, much of Genesis is taken up with the explanation of how Isaac and Jacob were kept from intermarrying with the peoples among whom they lived.

The last quarter of the book, which is occupied with the story of Joseph and his brethren, is designed to link these "fathers" and their God with the God and people of Moses. The same Jehovah who had once shown his power over Pharaoh for the protection of Abraham and Sarah, and who was later to show his power over another Pharaoh "who knew not Joseph," showed his power also over the Pharaoh of Joseph's day, in exalting Joseph from the dungeon to the post of highest honor and authority in Egypt, and in delivering Jacob and his whole family from death through Joseph's interposition. What their long residence in Egypt meant for God's people will be seen in another lesson.

QUESTIONS ON LESSON II

1. In what promise does God reveal to Abraham his plan to bless the world?
2. How was Abraham brought to believe in God's promise? What difference did it make whether he and his descendants believed it or not?
3. Did the patriarchs see that part of the promise fulfilled which gave them possession of "the Holy Land"? Read carefully Gen. 15 : 13–16 and Heb. 11 : 9, 10, 14–16.
4. Make a "family tree" in the usual way, showing those descendants of Terah who play any large part in the book of Genesis. Underscore in it the names of those men who were in the direct line of "the Promise."
5. How were Isaac and Jacob kept from marrying outside their own family?
6. Explain Joseph's words, "Ye meant evil against me; but God meant it for good, to bring to pass, as it is this day, to save much people alive." Gen. 50 : 20.

LESSON III
Egyptian Bondage and Deliverance

Exodus, Chapter 1

God says through his prophet Hosea, Hos. 11 : 1, "When Israel was a child, then I loved him, and called my son out of Egypt." See also Matt. 2 : 15. There was a loving, divine purpose in the Egyptian residence of God's people. What was it? What did this period mean in the career of Israel?

Most obviously, it meant growth. From the "seventy souls," Ex. 1 : 5, that went down into Egypt with Jacob, there sprang up there a populous folk, large enough to take its place alongside the other nations of the world of that day. Observe the nature of the land where this growth took place. Egypt was a settled country, where the twelve developing tribes could be united geographically and socially in a way impossible in a country like Palestine. However oppressed they were, they nevertheless were secluded from the dangers of raids from without and of civil strife within—just such dangers as later almost wrecked the substantial edifice slowly erected by this period of growth in Egypt.

Egypt meant also for Israel a time of waiting. All this growth was not accomplished in a short time. It lasted four hundred and thirty years. Ex. 12 : 40, 41. Through this long period, which seems like a dark tunnel between the brightness of the patriarchs' times and that of Moses' day, there was nothing for God's people to do but to wait. They were the heirs of God's promise, but they must wait for the fulfillment of that promise in God's own time, wait for a leader raised up by God, wait for the hour of national destiny to strike. As Hosea, ch.11: 1 expresses it, this "child" must wait for his Father's "call." The Egyptian period left an indelible impression on the mind of Israel. It formed the gray background on which God could lay the colors of his great deliverance. It is because God knew and planned this that he so often introduces himself to his people, when he speaks to them, as "Jehovah thy God, who brought thee out of the land of Egypt, out of the house of bondage."

In the third place, this Egyptian period meant for Israel a time of chastisement. The oppression to which the descendants of Jacob were exposed, when "there arose a new king over Egypt, who knew not

Joseph," Ex. 1 : 8, was so severe, prolonged, and hopeless, v. 14, that it has become proverbial and typical. Since every male child was to be put to death, v. 22, it is clear that the purpose of the Egyptians was nothing less than complete extermination. "It is good for a man that he bear the yoke in his youth": if that be true, then the children of Israel derived good from the school of discipline in which they grew up. True, as we read their later story, we feel that no people could be more fickle. Yet there is no other nation with which to compare Israel. And it is very probable that no other nation would have been serious-minded enough even to receive and grasp the divine revelation and leading of Moses' and Joshua's time. God, who had "seen the affliction of his people," who had "heard their cry" and sent Moses to them to organize their deliverance, wrote forever on this nation's soul the message of salvation in a historical record. At the start of their national life there stood the story, which they could never deny or forget, and which told them of God's power and grace.

Exodus, Chapters 5 to 15

All this lay in Israel's experience in Egypt. The next lesson will tell of the character and work of the man whom God chose to be leader. The means by which Moses succeeded in the seemingly impossible task of marching a great horde of slaves out from their masters' country, was the impression of God's power on the minds of Pharaoh and his people. It was a continued, combined, and cumulative impression. Of course it could not be made without the use of supernatural means. We must not, therefore, be surprised to find the story in Exodus bristling with miracles. To be sure, the "plagues" can be shown to be largely natural to that land where they occurred. And the supreme event of the deliverance, the passage of Israel through the Red Sea on dry ground, was due, according to the narrative itself, to a persistent wind, Ex. 14 : 21, such as often lays bare the shallows of a bay, only to release the waters again when its force is spent.

Nevertheless, it is not possible to remove the "hand of God" from the account by thus pointing out some of the means God used to accomplish his special purposes. It was at the time, in the way, and in the order, in which Moses announced to Pharaoh the arrival of the plagues, that they actually appeared. This was what had its ultimate effect on the king's stubborn will. And when Israel was told to "go forward," with the waters right before them, and when the Egyptians were saying, "They are entangled in the land, the wilderness hath shut them in," Ex. 14 : 3—it was just at that juncture that the east wind did its work at God's command; when Israel was over safely, it went down. Such things do not "happen." It made a profound impression on Israel, on Egypt, and on all the nations of that day; all united in accepting it as the work of Israel's God. Ex. 15 : 11, 14–16; Josh. 2 : 10.

The important point for the nation was to know, when Moses and Aaron came to them in the name of God, that it was their fathers' God who had sent them. On account of this need, which both the people and their leaders felt, God proclaimed his divine name, Jehovah (more precisely, *Yahweh*, probably meaning "He is," Ex. 3 : 14, 15), to Moses, and bade him pronounce the same to Israel, to assure them that he was "the God of Abraham, of Isaac, and of Jacob," and thus what Moses came now to do for them was just what had been promised to those fathers long before. The passover night was the fulfillment of God's good word to Abraham. Ex. 13 : 10, 11. How that word went on and on toward more and more complete fulfillment will be the subject of the succeeding lessons.

QUESTIONS ON LESSON III

1. What advantages had Egypt over Palestine as the place for Israel to grow from a family into a nation?
2. What value was there for Israel in a negative time of waiting at the beginning of its history?
3. Compare the effect on Israel with the effect on a man, of passing through a time of difficulty while developing.
4. Name the ten "plagues of Egypt" in their order. How far can they be called "natural"?
5. If the east wind drove back the Red Sea, what did God have to do with Israel's escape from the Egyptian army?
6. Why should we not be surprised to find many miracles grouped at this stage of Bible history?
7. How did God identify himself in the minds of the people with the God of their fathers? What was his personal name?

LESSON IV
Moses as Leader and Lawgiver

Exodus, Chapters 2 to 4

One of the things Israel had to wait for through those centuries in Egypt was a leader. When the time came God raised up such a leader for his people in Moses.

The story of how Moses' life was preserved in infancy, and of how he came to be brought up at the court of Pharaoh with all its advantages for culture, is one of the most fascinating tales of childhood. Ex. 2 : 1–10. But not many who know this familiar tale could go on with the biography of the man of forty who fled from Pharaoh's vengeance. Moses found by personal contact with his "brethren," the children of Israel, that they were not yet ready for common action, and would not easily acknowledge his right to lead them. After killing an Egyptian slave driver there was nothing for Moses to do but to flee. Vs. 11–15.

He spent the second forty years of his life, Acts 7 : 23, 30; Ex. 7 : 7, in the deserts about the eastern arm of the Red Sea—the region known to the Hebrews as Midian. There he married the daughter of the Midianite priest Reuel. (Jethro was probably Reuel's title, meaning "his excellency.") While herding his sheep in the mountains called Horeb (Sinai), Moses received at the burning bush that personal revelation of the God of his fathers, which lay at the base of all his future labors for God and his people. Ex. 3 : 1 to 4 : 17. It was a commission to lead Israel out of their bondage in Egypt into the land promised to their fathers.

Though very humble as to his fitness for such leadership, Moses was assured of Jehovah's presence and help. He was equipped with extraordinary powers for convincing the proud Pharaoh that his demands were God's demands; and he was given the aid of his brother Aaron, who had a readiness of speech which Moses at this time seems to have lacked.

Exodus, Chapters 16 to 24

How the two brothers achieved the seemingly impossible task of winning out of Egypt, and of uniting a spiritless and unorganized mass of slaves upon a desperate enterprise, is the narrative that fills the early chapters of Exodus. But with Israel safe across the Red

Sea, Moses' leadership had only begun. He instituted an organization of the people for relieving himself of his heavy duties as judge. He determined the line of march, and sustained the spirits of the fighting men in their struggle against the tribes of the desert who challenged Israel's passage.

But, above all, Moses became the "mediator" of the "covenant," Heb. 9 : 19–21, between the Hebrews and Jehovah their God at Mount Sinai. On the basis of the Ten Commandments, Ex. 20 : 2–17; Deut. 5 : 6–21, that guide to God's nature and will which formed the Hebrew constitution, the people agreed to worship and obey Jehovah alone, and Jehovah promised to be their God, fulfilling to them his promises made to their fathers. By solemn sacrifices, according to the custom of the time, when the symbolism of altar and priesthood was well understood, this covenant was sealed.

Exodus, Chapter 25 to Numbers, Chapter 36

After long seclusion on the mount alone with God, Moses ordered the erection of a house of worship. It had to be portable, so as to accompany them in their wanderings and express visibly, wherever set up, the religious unity of the twelve tribes. Aaron and his sons were consecrated to be the official priesthood of this new shrine and were clothed and instructed accordingly. Minute details regulated all sacrifices, and similar minute instructions enabled the priests to decide questions of ceremonial cleanness and uncleanness in matters of food and health.

All these laws and regulations, mainly recorded in Leviticus, were given through Moses, either alone or in association with his brother. It is not surprising to learn that there were those who challenged this exclusive leadership in every department of the national life. We read of a willful disregard of divine orders even in the family of Aaron, with immediate fatal results. Lev. 10 : 1–7. Like punishment overtook those members of the tribe of Levi who showed jealousy of the house of Aaron, and those elements in other tribes that claimed rights equal or superior to those of Moses. Num., chs. 16, 17. It would be strange, indeed, if God, who had vindicated his servant Moses against Pharaoh, should let his own authority as represented by Moses be challenged within the camp of Israel. He punished to save.

Just as God took up the Sabbath and circumcision, old customs of the preceding era, into the law of Israel, so also he spoke to this people through an elaborate system of feasts and pilgrimages, which bound up their whole year with the worship of God. Indeed, the principle of the seventh part of time as sacred was extended to the seventh year, and even to the fiftieth year (the year following the seventh seven), for beneficent social and economic uses. Lev., ch. 25.

When at length the nation, thus organized and equipped, set forth from Sinai, Num. 10 : 11, they required a leadership of a different kind—military leadership and practical statesmanship. They found both in Moses. He it was who led them through all the long wanderings in the peninsula of Sinai, bearing their murmurings and meeting their recurrent difficulties with a patience that seems almost divine, save for that one lapse which was to cost him and Aaron their entrance into the Promised Land. Num. 20 : 10–12.

At the border of the land, from the top of Pisgah in the long mountain wall of Moab, Moses at last looked down into that deep gorge of the Jordan Valley at his feet, which separated him from the hills of Canaan. Beyond this river and the Dead Sea, into which it empties, lay the land long ago promised to the seed of Abraham. Moses had been permitted to lead the people to its very gateway; but it remained for another, his younger helper, Joshua, to lead them through the gate into the house of rest.

The Book of Deuteronomy

But before he surrendered his power to another and his life to his Maker, the aged Moses rehearsed in the ears of Israel the great principles of God's law. He pleaded earnestly with them to accept it from the heart, to adapt it to the changed conditions of their new settled life with its new temptations, and to hand it down as their most precious heritage to their children after them. This is the purpose and substance of the book of Deuteronomy, which gets its name from the fact that it is a "second lawgiving." It is the Law of Sinai repeated, but in oratorical form, charged with the feeling and spirit of that "man of God," whose name is forever linked with the Law and with the God who gave it to mankind.

QUESTIONS ON LESSON IV

1. How did Moses' forty years in Egypt and his forty years in Midian help to prepare him for leadership?
2. What was the constitution of the new Hebrew State established at Sinai? How was it ratified?

3. How was the tabernacle suited to the religious needs of Israel during Moses' lifetime?
4. Show how the Law of Moses takes up the old principle of the Sabbath and applies it to the life of Israel.
5. Where did Moses' leadership end, and what was his last service to the nation?

LESSON V
The Conquest and Settlement of Canaan
The Book of Joshua

On the death of Aaron his son, Eleazar, succeeded him as high priest. But when Moses died, it was not a son who succeeded him in the political and moral leadership of Israel, for that position was not hereditary. Joshua, a man of Ephraim, was divinely designated for this work. He was fitted for the difficult undertaking by military experience, Ex. 17 : 9–14, by personal acquaintance with Canaan, Num. 13 : 8, 16; 14 : 6, 30, 38, and by long and intimate association with Moses, Ex. 33 : 11; Num. 11 : 28; Deut. 34 : 9; Josh. 1 : 1. The book of Joshua, which records his career, divides naturally into two parts, first, the conquest, chs. 1 to 12, and second, the settlement, chs. 13 to 22. Two further chapters, chs. 23, 24, contain Joshua's valedictory address.

Before Moses' death two and a half tribes had already received their assignment of territory on the east of the Jordan, out of lands conquered from the Amorite kings, Sihon and Og. But the fighting men of these tribes agreed to accompany the other tribes and share their struggle till all had obtained an inheritance. So when the great host passed over the Jordan, not far from where it empties into the Dead Sea, the men of Reuben, Gad, and Manasseh crossed with the rest. Jehovah, who at the Red Sea a generation earlier had struck terror into the hearts of all nations by his wonderful interposition to save Israel and destroy its enemies, repeated here his saving help, by stemming the swift current of the Jordan River, till all had passed over dry shod to the western side.

Once over, they found themselves face to face with Jericho, a city which commanded the passes into the mountain country beyond. Spies previously despatched to learn the weakness of Jericho had reported the panic of its inhabitants and so prepared the Hebrews to believe God's word, when through Joshua he announced a bloodless victory here at the beginning of their conquest. Without a blow struck Jericho fell, and all its inhabitants were "devoted," at Jehovah's strict command. Even their wealth was to be "devoted," that is, the cattle slain and the goods added to the treasury of the sanctuary. Only Rahab, who had saved the spies, and her family were excepted. One man, Achan, disobeyed the ban on private spoils. His covetousness and deception, revealed by Israel's defeat in the expedition against Ai which followed the fall of Jericho, and detected by the use of the sacred lot, was punished by the execution of all who were privy to the crime.

Better success attended the second attempt to take Ai. With these two cities reduced, Jericho at the bottom and Ai at the top of the valley leading up from the Jordan floor to the central highland, Joshua was in a position to attack anywhere without fear of being outflanked. Middle, south, and north was the order commended by military considerations. Accordingly those cities which, because in the middle of the land, felt themselves the most immediately threatened, took the first steps to avert the menace. A group of five towns lying just north of Jerusalem, with Gibeon at their head, succeeded by a ruse in getting a treaty of peace from Joshua. The Gibeonites deceived Joshua by representing themselves as having come from a great distance to seek an alliance. Joshua's pride was flattered and he fell a victim to the trick. The consequences were serious, for these Canaanites, though reduced to vassalage, remained as aliens in the heart of the land, and cut off the southern from the northern tribes of Israel.

A confederacy of the chief cities in the region south of Gibeon, headed by the king of Jerusalem, determined to strike the first blow. But their campaign against the Gibeonites, now the allies of Israel, ended in a quick advance by Joshua and his complete subjugation of all these cities, the humiliation and death of their kings, and the "devotion" of the inhabitants who fell into his hands.

A similar campaign followed in the north, with the city of Hazor at the head of the Canaanite forces. At the "waters of Merom," a small lake a few miles north of the Sea of Galilee, a surprise attack by Joshua deprived his enemies of their advantage in horsemen and chariots on the level ground they had selected for battle, and resulted in the utter rout of the Canaanites and the general slaughter of every soul that did not escape by flight from the "devoted" towns.

Thus from Mount Hermon on the north to the wilderness of the wandering on the south, the whole land had been swept over and reduced to impotence by the Hebrew invader. It was time to apportion it now to the several tribes. This was accomplished under the direction of Joshua and Eleazar. Judah and Joseph, the two strongest tribes, were assigned, the one to the south and the other to the north of the main mountain mass. Levi's inheritance was to be "the Lord," that is, the religious tithes, and his dwelling was to be "among his brethren," that is, in designated towns throughout all the land. A commission of three representatives from each of the seven other western tribes divided the rest of the conquered territory into seven fairly equal parts. These then were assigned to the seven tribes by lot at the tabernacle at Shiloh. As for the eastern tribes, when they returned to their homes across the Jordan, they built an altar at the ford, as a permanent "witness" to the unity of all the sons of Jacob, however the deep gorge of the Jordan might cut them off from one another.

At Shechem, where Abraham built his first altar in Canaan, Joshua had renewed the covenant between the people and their God as soon as he had secured control of Mount Ephraim, the middle highlands. He had not only read the Law of Moses to all the people here, but also inscribed it on stones for the sake of permanence and publicity. And now, when the conquest was complete and Joshua was nearing his end, he reassembled the people at the same spot, to remind them there of that solemn covenant, and to leave with them his final charge of fidelity to their God and his one central sanctuary.

QUESTIONS ON LESSON V

1. How was Joshua specially fitted to succeed Moses as leader of Israel?
2. Which tribes received their inheritance east of the Jordan? How did these show their sense of the unity of all Israel (a) at the beginning, and (b) at the close of the conquest?
3. What justification can be urged for the stern measures which Israel took with the Canaanites and their possessions?
4. What was the plan of Joshua's campaign, and what relation did the capture of Jericho and Ai bear to it?
5. How did the men of Gibeon deceive Joshua, and why? What lasting damage was caused by his treaty with them?
6. Locate on a map the inheritance of each of the tribes.

LESSON VI
The Period of the Judges
The Books of Judges and Ruth

In Egypt, Israel had grown from a family into a folk. In the wilderness the folk had become a nation. In the conquest the nation had gotten its home. But in the period of the Judges which followed the conquest this steady advance seemed interrupted. What do we find at this time?

We find a loose confederacy of tribes, aware of their common origin, yet too jealous of local names and rights to combine for a common end, too selfish to help one another until the danger of one has become a tragedy for all.

The nature of the land the Hebrews had occupied helped this divisive tendency. The great gash of the Jordan Valley, its bed two or three thousand feet below the mountain country on either side, cut off the eastern minority from the western majority. In the west a plain separated the foothills of the central range from the seashore. This plain not only contained enemies like the Philistines whom only a united Israel could have conquered, but also quickly altered the type of its Hebrew settlers. Right across the mountain belt from the sea to the Jordan stretched an almost unbroken plain (Esdraelon), varying from sea level to the lower level of the Jordan. This cut off the mountaineers to the north (Galilee) from those to the south (Ephraim). And a glance at any physical map will show how even in the mountain country deep, lateral valleys reach up from either side so far toward the center that communication from north to south is only by a series of violent grades, save along that narrow ridge in the middle where runs the highroad between Hebron, Jerusalem, Shechem, and Jezreel.

Under these conditions only some strong positive force could prevent the disintegration of the Hebrew nation. Such a force the religion of Jehovah was intended to be, and would have been, if the people had remained faithful to it. It had one high priest, descendant of Aaron, and associated therefore with all the memories of Moses and Sinai. It had a single sanctuary, the seat of Ark and oracle, the center of pilgrimage three times a year. It had one law for all Hebrews, a law far superior to the codes of all other nations, and revealing the nature and will of a single moral and spiritual deity. All this provided the focus for a mighty nation, with a pure "theocracy," that is, a government by God himself. But the people did not remain faithful. They fell away in this time of the Judges.

The Book of Judges, which tells the story of this period, records a long list of names, each one connected with some particular enemy of Israel, some tribe or group of tribes delivered, and some definite term of years during which the deliverer "judged" the people. On this list the most conspicuous names are those of Deborah and of Gideon in the north, of Jephthah east of the Jordan (Gilead), and of Samson in the south. Most of the other judges are little more than names to us. Deborah stands out, not only because she was a woman, but also for her wonderful "song" preserved in the fifth chapter, celebrating Barak's victory over the Canaanites near Mount Carmel. Gideon is memorable for his strategems and his persistence, and for his near approach to a real kingship, which was offered to him and his house after his victory, but which he declined, saying, "Jehovah shall rule over you." Ch. 8 : 23. His son Abimelech was actually termed king in and around the city of Shechem for a few years, but perished miserably for his sins. Ch. 9 : 6, 56. Jephthah's career was mainly concerned with the region east of the Jordan, but his admirable "apology" for Israel showed his sense of Hebrew solidarity. Samson's picturesque story, with its petty loves and hates, its riddles and its practical jokes, ended in a sacrificial death which in part redeems its meanness. But neither Samson nor any of his predecessors accomplished anything permanent.

Two words of caution belong to the study of this book and of these times. First, we must not suppose that one judge necessarily follows another in point of time because his story follows the other's story in the book. Judges 10 : 7 shows that oppressions of different sections of the land by different enemies might be taking place at the same time, and suggests that the figures assigned to each judge at the close of his story cannot safely be added together to find the total length of this period. And second, those figures themselves (nearly always forty or eighty) are to be taken as "round numbers," rather than as precise data such as we look for to-day to make out a table of chronology. In the same way the four hundred and eighty years of I Kings 6 : 1 is evidently intended as twelve times forty years, to represent the whole time from the Exodus to Solomon. For when we have subtracted from the beginning of it one forty-year term for the wanderings, and from the end of it three forty-year terms for Eli, I Sam. 4 : 18, Saul, Acts 13 : 21, and David, I Kings 2 : 11, then we have left eight forty-year terms for the Judges. Eight times forty is three hundred and twenty. Those three hundred and twenty years would then correspond with the three hundred years mentioned by Jephthah in Judg. 11 : 26 as dividing Moses' days from his own. Under these circumstances we are wise to wait for further light from archæology before fixing the precise date of any one of these interesting persons,

There are three additions or appendices to the Book of Judges. The first of them, including chs. 17, 18, tells how the Danites came to live in the extreme north, and the origin of the idolatrous sanctuary at that city of Dan which was reckoned as the northern limit of Canaan— "from Dan to Beer-sheba." The second occupies the three remaining chapters of Judges, and records the civil war between Benjamin and the other tribes on account of "the sin of Gibeah," Hos. 10 : 9. And the third appendix is the story of Ruth the Moabitess which now makes a separate book in the Bible. Besides its inherent charm the story claims special notice because of the light it throws on that Bethlehem family which was soon to furnish the nation its great king, David.

QUESTIONS ON LESSON VI

1. What influences made for the loss of Hebrew unity as soon as Joshua's generation was dead?
2. What forces remained to bind the tribes together? Why did not these forces suffice?
3. How were the persons selected who ruled Israel in this period? Were they "judges" in the same sense as our judges to-day? What besides?
4. What three groups of tribes tended to draw together under common leaders? Tell the exploits of one distinguished judge belonging to each of these groups.
5. With what reserve should we use the figures in this book to construct a chronology of the period?
6. Point out the relation of the book of Ruth to the closing portion of the Book of Judges. What lends Ruth peculiar historical interest?

LESSON VII
Samuel and Saul: Prophecy and Monarchy
The First Book of Samuel

Sometimes Eli and sometimes Samuel are called the last of the Judges. But neither of these was a judge in the same exclusive sense as Gideon or Samson. Eli was the high priest, but exercised the office of judge for his time. Samuel was a prophet, who also "judged Israel" in the interval between Eli's death and Saul's accession. Both men mark the time of transition between the period of the Judges and the monarchy. And the two names are most closely linked, for it was under Eli's instruction, at the sanctuary in Shiloh, that Samuel grew up.

The story of Hannah and her dedication of her little son to God as a "Nazirite," I Sam. 1 : 11; compare Num. 6 : 1–8, to dwell all his life at the house of God, I Sam. 1 : 28, has a peculiar charm for young and old. It gives a picture of personal piety in a rude age, and thus serves to correct our idea of the times. Beginning at a very early age, I Sam. 3 : 1 to 4 : 1, Samuel became the chosen and recognized mouthpiece of Israel's God.

That is the essential meaning of a prophet—one who speaks for God. Exodus 4 : 16 is instructive, for it shows that as Aaron was to be "a mouth" to Moses, while Moses was "as God" to Aaron, so the prophet was God's mouthpiece or spokesman. Of course a prophet was often a person who also spoke before—one, that is, who predicted what should come to pass. And the fact that his words were actually fulfilled became a proof of his divine commission, both in theory, Deut. 18 : 22, and in practice, Isa. 44 : 26. But the bulk of the prophets' messages were, like those of Samuel, addressed to their own time. They were preachers of righteousness, warners against sin, the nation's conscience, and the Lord's remembrancers.

It is the chief glory of Samuel that he was not only first in the long line of the Hebrew prophets—the most remarkable succession of men the world has ever seen—but also the founder of the prophetic order. By the prophetic order we mean the prophets as a group conscious of their solidarity, the identity of their principles and aim. Samuel gathered about his dominating personality those persons who were sympathetic with him in spirit, and who shared with him some of that power of testimony which "the word of Jehovah" conferred. They seem to have lived together, I Sam. 19 : 20, in communities similar to those two centuries later under Elijah and Elisha. They used musical instruments in their devotions, which were public as well as private. Ch. 10 : 5. They were the center of patriotic zeal as well as of religious effort. In fact, the belief in Israel's God was so evidently the bond that bound Israel together, that for the common man patriotism and religion were in danger of being regarded as one and the same thing.

It is not surprising, therefore, that out of Samuel's time and from the forces which Samuel set in motion, there came two movements which changed the course of the nation's history: an outward movement for independence, and an inward movement for monarchy. A revival of religion could not fail to rouse the subjected Hebrews against their oppressors, the Philistines. The reverses they suffered in battle against their better armed and better led enemies put it into their minds to set up a king, "like all the nations."

Samuel, as the national leader, was God's agent in selecting, consecrating, and establishing the first king. He chose Saul, of the tribe of Benjamin, a man of heroic proportions though of modest demeanor. Ch. 9 : 2, 21. His choice met the popular approval, at first with general and outward acquiescence, though with much inward reserve and individual revolt; but after his first successful campaign with universal loyalty. Ch. 10 : 27; 11 : 12–15.

That first military effort of the new monarch was against the Ammonites. But a greater test remained in the menace of the Philistines, whose garrisons at strategic points in the mountains of Israel served to keep the tribes in check. Under those circumstances Saul was cautious, for he had but a small force, inadequately armed, at his disposal. But the initiative, for which all Israel waited, was taken by Saul's son, Jonathan. Unknown to his father, Jonathan, accompanied only by his armor-bearer, but encouraged by an indication of God's will and by the enemy's slackness, ch. 14 : 12, attacked boldly a Philistine garrison that relied too much on the natural strength of its position. He began in this way a panic in the enemy's ranks, and soon drew after him in pursuit of them not only Saul's small army but multitudes of Hebrews who in their hiding places only waited such a signal to fall upon the hated oppressor. The victory of Michmash was overwhelming, the mountain country was cleared of the Philistines, and an independent people began to enjoy the reign of their first king.

Unhappily Saul did not prove himself so well equipped for the kingship in character and disposition as in personal prowess. Jealousy, natural in a king whose claim to authority was so new and weak, was heightened in Saul by a malady that induced fits of sullenness and rage. His humility and modesty of other days gave place to envy, vanity, and cruelty. Even God's express commands through the same prophet on whose divine commission Saul's claim to the throne rested were not heeded, for Samuel had to rebuke him for disobedience and only refrained from publicly rejecting him at Saul's abject entreaty. Ch. 15 : 30.

Room was found in Saul's heart for jealousy of the popularity and success of David, ch. 18 : 8, the young man of Bethlehem in Judah whom at first he had loved and attached to his person, ch. 16 : 21. Jonathan, though heir to his father's throne and aware that David had been designated as Jehovah's choice for king, ch. 20 : 15, 31, had nothing but affection for David his friend. But Saul pursued David openly, after failing in repeated secret attempts to make away with him. And the close of Saul's life is marred by his vindictive pursuit of his rival, till death in battle with the Philistines at Mount Gilboa brought the first king of Israel to a miserable end and left the way open for David to become his successor.

QUESTIONS ON LESSON VII

1. Who shares with Samuel the leadership of Israel in the time of transition from the judges to the kings, and what relation did he bear to Samuel?
2. What was a prophet, what is meant by the prophetic order, and what is Samuel's particular service and distinction among the prophets?
3. What motive led to the popular demand for a king, and how did Samuel as God's representative regard this demand?
4. Sketch the character of Saul. What was his achievement for Israel? Wherein did he fail?
5. Compare Saul and Jonathan in ability and character.

LESSON VIII
David and Solomon: Psalms and Wisdom

**The Second Book of Samuel; I Kings, Chapters 1 to 11;
I Chronicles, Chapter 10 to II Chronicles, Chapter 9**

One of Saul's sons, Ish-bosheth, for a short time after the death of his father and brothers in battle, attempted to maintain his right to succeed Saul on the throne. But when Abner, his kinsman and the head of the army, turned to David, son of Jesse, who was already reigning at Hebron as king over Judah, all the tribes followed him. Both Ish-bosheth and Abner soon perished.

With his new dignity David promptly acquired a new capital, better suited than Hebron in location and strength to be the nation's center. He captured the fortress of Jebus, five miles north of Bethlehem, his old home, from its Canaanitish defenders, and enlarged, strengthened, and beautified it. Under its ancient name of Jerusalem he made it both the political and the religious capital of Israel.

The Ark of the Covenant, which in Eli's time had been captured by the Philistines, had been returned by them, and for many years had rested in a private house, was regarded as the very heart and symbol of the national religion. David therefore brought it first to Jerusalem, and instead of uniting with it its former housing, the old Mosaic tabernacle, he gave it a temporary home in a tent, intending to build a splendid temple when he should have peace. But war continued through the days of David, and at God's direction the erection of a temple, save for certain preparations, was left to Solomon, David's successor.

David was victorious in war. His success showed itself in the enlargement of Israel's boundaries, the complete subjection—for the time—of all alien elements in the land, and the alliance with Hiram, king of Tyre, with the great building operations which this alliance made possible. A royal palace formed the center of a court such as other sovereigns maintained, and David's court and even his family were exposed to the same corrupting influences as power, wealth, jealousy, and faction have everywhere introduced. Absalom, his favorite son, ill requited his father's love and trust by organizing a revolt against him. It failed, but not until it had driven the king, now an old man, into temporary exile and had let loose civil war upon the land.

Solomon, designated by David to succeed him, did not gain the throne without dispute, but the attempt of Adonijah, another son, to seize the throne failed in spite of powerful support. The forty-year reign of Solomon was the golden age of Hebrew history—the age to which all subsequent times looked back. Rapid growth of commerce, construction, art, and literature reflected the inward condition of peace and the outward ties with other lands of culture. But with art came idolatry; with construction came ostentation and oppression; with commerce came luxury. The splendor of Jerusalem, wherein Solomon "made silver . . . to be as stones, and cedars . . . as the sycomore-trees," I Kings 10 : 27, contained in itself the seeds of dissolution.

However, there are two great types of literature which found their characteristic expression in the days of David and Solomon and are always associated with their names—the psalm with David, and the proverb (or, more broadly, "wisdom") with Solomon. Kingdom, temple and palace have long since passed away, but the Psalter and the books of Wisdom are imperishable monuments of the united monarchy.

The Psalms

The Psalter is a collection of one hundred and fifty poems, of various length, meter, and style. As now arranged it is divided into five books, but there is evidence that earlier collections and arrangements preceded the present. Among the earliest productions, judged both by form and by matter, are those psalms which bear the superscription "of David," though it would not be safe to assert that every such psalm came from David's own pen or that none not so labeled is not of Davidic origin. Judged alike from the narrative in the book of Samuel, and from the traditions scattered in other books as early as Amos, ch. 6 : 5, and as late as Chronicles, I Chron. 15 : 16 to 16 : 43; ch. 25, David was both a skilled musician himself and an organizer of music for public worship. It is not surprising, therefore, to find a body of religious poems ascribed to him, which not only evidence his piety and good taste, but also, though individual in tone, are well-adapted to common use at the sanctuary.

The psalms are poems. Their poetry is not simply one of substance, but also a poetry of form. Rime, our familiar device, is of course absent, but there is rhythm, although it is not measured in the same strict way as in most of our poetry. The most striking and characteristic mark of Hebrew poetic form is the parallel structure: two companion lines serve together to complete a single thought, as the second either repeats, supplements, emphasizes, illustrates, or contrasts with the first.

Proverbs; Job; Ecclesiastes

Poetry is also a term to which the book of Proverbs and most of the other productions of "Wisdom" are entitled. While they are chiefly didactic (that is, intended for instruction) instead of lyric (emotional self-expression), nevertheless the Wisdom books are almost entirely written in rhythmic parallelism and contain much matter unsuited to ordinary prose expression. In the Revised Version the manner of printing shows to the English reader at a glance what parts are prose and what are poetry (compare, for example, Job, ch. 2 with Job, ch. 3), though it must be admitted that a hard and fast line cannot be drawn between them. Compare Eccl., ch. 7 with Proverbs.

"The wise," as a class of public teachers in the nation (see Jer. 18 : 18), associated their beginnings with King Solomon (Prov. 24 : 23; 25 : 1), whose wisdom is testified to in the book of Kings, as well as his speaking of "proverbs," that is, pithy sayings easy to remember and teach, mostly of moral import. I Kings 4 : 29-34. But the profoundest theme of wisdom was the moral government of God as seen in his works and ways. The mysteries with which all men, to-day as well as in ancient times, must grapple when they seek to harmonize their faith in a just and good God with such undeniable facts as prosperous sinners and suffering saints, led to the writing of such books as Job (the meaning of a good man's adversities) and Ecclesiastes (the vanity of all that mere experience and observation of life afford). In the case of these Wisdom books, as in that of the Psalms, the oldest name—that of the royal founder—is not to be taken as the exclusive author. Solomon, like David, made the beginnings; others collected, edited, developed, and completed.

QUESTIONS ON LESSON VIII

1. In what tribe and town did David first reign as king? How did he secure a new capital when he became king of all Israel? How and why did he make this the religious capital also?

2. What advantages and disadvantages did David's continual wars, and his imitation of other kings' courts, bring to him, his family, and his people?
3. What was David's part in the development of religious poetry? How does Hebrew poetry differ generally from English poetry in form? Name the books of the Old Testament written chiefly or wholly in poetry.
4. Who built the first Temple? Who were "the wise" in Israel, whom did they venerate as their royal patron, and what did they aim to accomplish by their writings?

LESSON IX
The Kingdom of Israel

I Kings, Chapter 12 to II Kings, Chapter 17

With the death of Solomon came the lasting division of the tribes into two kingdoms, a northern and a southern, known as the Kingdom of Israel and the Kingdom of Judah. Rehoboam on his accession announced a policy of repression and even oppression that alienated completely the loyalty of Ephraim and the other northern tribes, which were never attached to the house of David in the same way as the tribe of Judah was. Under a man of Ephraim, therefore, Jeroboam the son of Nebat, who in earlier years had challenged even Solomon's title, the ten tribes revolted from Rehoboam and established a separate state.

Rehoboam found himself too weak to prevent this secession, and he and his descendants of David's dynasty had to content themselves with the narrow boundaries of Judah. To be sure, in Jerusalem they possessed the authorized center of public worship for the whole nation. It was to offset this advantage that Jeroboam made Bethel, that spot associated in the minds of the people with the patriarchs themselves, his religious capital. And, influenced perhaps by the Egyptian example of steer worship (for he had long lived as a fugitive in Egypt in Solomon's reign), he made golden steers and placed them in the sanctuary at Bethel and in that at Dan in the extreme north. (See close of Lesson VI.) To these places and under these visible symbols of brute force, Jeroboam summoned his people to worship Jehovah. It was the old national religion but in the degraded form of an image worship forbidden by the Mosaic Commandments.

A throne thus built on mere expediency could not endure. Jeroboam's son was murdered after a two years' reign. Nor did this usurper succeed in holding the throne for his house any longer than Jeroboam's house had lasted. At length Omri, commander of the army, succeeded in founding a dynasty that furnished four kings. Ahab, son of Omri, who held the throne the longest of these four, is the king with whom we become best acquainted of all the northern monarchs. This is partly because of the relations between Ahab and Elijah the prophet. Ahab's name is also linked with that of his queen, the notorious Jezebel, a princess of Tyre, who introduced the worship of the Tyrian Baal into Israel and even persecuted all who adhered to the national religion.

This alliance with Tyre, and the marriage of Ahab's daughter to a prince of Judah, secured Israel on the north and the south, and left Ahab free to pursue his father's strong policy toward the peoples to the east, Moab and Syria. Upon Ahab's death in battle against Syria, Moab revolted, and the two sons of Ahab, in spite of help from the house of David in Jerusalem, were unable to stave off the ruin that threatened the house of Omri. Jehu, supported by the army in which he was a popular leader, seized the throne, with the usual assassination of all akin to the royal family. His inspiration to revolt had been due to Jehovah's prophets, and his program was the overthrow of Baal worship in favor of the old national religion. Though Jehu thoroughly destroyed the followers of Jezebel's foreign gods, he and his sons after him continued to foster the idolatrous shrines at Bethel and Dan, so that the verdict of the sacred writer upon them is unfavorable: they "departed not from all the sins of Jeroboam the son of Nebat, wherewith he made Israel to sin."

Mesha, king of Moab, II Kings 3 : 4, lived long enough to see his oppressors, the kings of Omri's house, overthrown and the land of Israel reduced to great weakness. (See article "Moabite Stone" in any Bible dictionary.) Jehu's son, Jehoahaz, witnessed the deepest humiliation of Israel at the hands of Syria. But it was not many years after Mesha's boasting that affairs took a complete turn. Jehu's grandson, Jehoash, spurred by Elisha the prophet even on his deathbed, began the recovery which attained its zenith in the reign of Jeroboam II, fourth king of Jehu's line. Though little is told of this reign in the Book of Kings, it is clear that at no time since Solomon's reign had a king of Israel ruled over so large a territory. It was the last burst of glory before total extinction.

There is a history lying between the reigns of Jeroboam I, founder of the Northern Kingdom, and of Jeroboam II, its last prosperous monarch, which has scarcely been referred to in this brief sketch of its kings. It is the history of Jehovah's prophets.

Hosea; Amos; Jonah

Reference has already been made to the rise of the prophetic order as such, in the time of Samuel. (Lesson VII.) With each crisis in the affairs of the nation God raised up some notable messenger with a word from him to the people or to the ruler. But all along the fire of devotion to God and country was kept alive by humbler, unnamed men, who supplied a sound nucleus of believers even to this Northern Kingdom with its idolatrous shrines and its usurping princes. I Kings 18 : 4; 19 : 18.

The greatest names are those of Elijah and Elisha. The earlier struggle to keep Israel true to Jehovah focuses in these two men, one the worthy successor of the other. Their time marked perhaps the lowest ebb of true religion in all the history of God's Kingdom on earth. It is no wonder, therefore, that such stern, strong men were not only raised up to fight for the God of Moses and Samuel and David, but also endowed with exceptional powers, to work wonders and signs for the encouragement of the faithful and the confounding of idolators and sinners. Such was the purpose of their notable miracles.

Elijah and Elisha wrote nothing. But in their spirit rose up Hosea and Amos a century later—men who have left a record of their prophecies in the books that bear their names. Denunciation of sin, especially in the higher classes, announcement of impending punishment for that sin, and promise of a glorious, if distant, future of pardon, peace, and prosperity through God's grace and man's sincere repentance— these things form the substance of their eloquent messages. Hosea is noteworthy for his striking parable of a patient husband and a faithless wife to illustrate God's love and Israel's infidelity. Amos, himself a herdsman from Judah sent north to denounce a king and people not his own, is startling in the suddenness with which he turns the popular religious ideas against those who harbor them. See, for example, ch. 3 : 2, where Amos makes the unique relation between Jehovah and Israel the reason, not for Israel's safety from Jehovah's wrath, as the people thought, but for the absolute certainty of Israel's punishment for all its sins. These two prophets, the last of the Northern

Kingdom, had the melancholy duty of predicting the utter overthrow of what the first Jeroboam had set up in rebellion and sin two centuries before.

QUESTIONS ON LESSON IX

1. When, why, and under whose lead did the ten tribes break away from the house of David?
2. Outline the fortunes of the kings of Israel from Jeroboam I to Jeroboam II.
3. Who were the outstanding prophets in the Northern Kingdom, and what was the substance of their messages?

LESSON X

The Kingdom of Judah, to Hezekiah

I Kings, Chapter 12 to II Kings, Chapter 17; II Chronicles, Chapters 10 to 28; Obadiah; Joel; Micah; Isaiah (in part)

The revolt of Jeroboam and the ten northern tribes reduced the dominion ruled by Rehoboam, grandson of David, to narrow bounds. Before his disastrous reign was over, Judah was still further humiliated by an invasion under Shishak, a Pharaoh of the twenty-second dynasty of Egypt, who despoiled Jerusalem of the treasures which Solomon had amassed. After the death of Rehoboam and the short reign of his son, Abijam, Judah was ruled successively by Asa and Jehoshaphat, each succeeding his father peacefully and each reigning long and, on the whole, prosperously. Another invasion from the south which threatened to be as disastrous as that of Shishak, under "Zerah the Ethiopian" was repelled by Asa. Internal reforms, both religious and civil, were carried out by these vigorous rulers.

The natural rivalry and intermittent warfare between north and south, which had arisen through the division under Rehoboam, ceased for a time after Jehoshaphat entered into alliance with King Ahab and took Athaliah, Ahab's daughter, as wife for his son Joram. The kings of Samaria and Jerusalem made common cause against Syria and Moab, and a temporary success seemed to crown the new policy. But prophets of Jehovah repeatedly warned the king who sat on David's throne of the danger to the true religion from such an alliance with Baal worshipers,

It was not long before their warnings were justified by the facts. Athaliah, Joram's queen, was the daughter not only of Ahab but also of Jezebel and brought with her to Jerusalem the fierce spirit and heathen habits of her Tyrian mother. King Ahaziah her son lost his life through his close association with King Jehoram of Israel, his uncle, for Jehu made away with both kings at the same time, and with all the princes of Judah, kinsmen of Ahaziah, on whom he could lay his hands. The old tigress at Jerusalem, Athaliah, now turned upon her own flesh and blood, the children of Ahaziah, and murdered them all so as to secure the power for herself. One grandson alone, the infant Joash, escaped, saved by an aunt who hid him and his nurse from the cruel queen mother. Six years later this child was proclaimed king in the Temple courts by Jehoiada, the high priest. Athaliah was slain, and a new era began in Judah with the destruction of Baal worship and the repair of Jehovah's Temple.

Joash was too weak to do more than buy off the king of Syria when his army threatened Jerusalem, and he himself met his death in a conspiracy. The same fate befell his son Amaziah, after a reign that promised well but was wrecked on the king's ambition to subdue the Northern Kingdom under him. Uzziah (or Azariah) succeeded to the throne, though for half of his long reign he and his kingdom seem to have been in a state of vassalage to Jeroboam II, the powerful ruler of Israel. The latter part of Uzziah's reign was more prosperous, in spite of the king's pitiable state—for he was stricken with leprosy and had to live apart. It was on this account that he associated his son Jotham with himself, and during the sixteen years of Jotham's reign—most of which was included within the long nominal reign of Uzziah—the Philistines, Ammonites, and Arabians were defeated in warfare, while considerable building both in and out of the capital helped to prepare the little kingdom for the troublous days just ahead.

The mighty kingdom of Assyria, with its capital at Nineveh on the Tigris River, was the force which God used to punish his faithless people. Lying beyond the kingdoms of Syria, Israel's nearest neighbors on the north, Assyria was not at first felt to be the menace which in the end it proved to be. Whenever Assyria was strong, Syria was weak, and the king in Samaria could breathe freely. But there came a day when a king of unusual power ascended the throne at Nineveh, Tiglath-pileser (or Pul, as he was also called, see II Kings 15 : 19, 29), and the fate of both Syria and Israel was sealed.

Ahaz, the son of Jotham who had just died, saw in this Assyrian the means of delivering Judah out of the hands of Pekah, king of Israel, and Rezin, king of Syria, who had joined forces to capture Jerusalem and put a king of their own on the throne of David. By a great present Ahaz bought the support of Tiglath-pileser, who sent an army to attack Judah's foes. Syria was devastated, the inhabitants were carried away captive from all the eastern and northern parts of Israel (Gilead and Galilee), Phœnicia and Philistia were overrun, and Ahaz, among other kings, went to Damascus in person to do homage to this irresistible conqueror.

In the Northern Kingdom, reduced now to little more than the central highlands of Ephraim and Manasseh, Hoshea, a protegé of the Assyrian king, reigned for a few years. But he and his foolish advisers, unable to read the signs of the times, looked to Egypt for help and revolted. This time the end had come. Shalmaneser, now on the Assyrian throne, came against Samaria, and after a siege lasting almost three years, took and destroyed it. The whole population was carried away, after the drastic policy of deportation practiced by Assyria, and an alien population was introduced to take their places. Thus ended the Northern Kingdom after lasting a little over two centuries. And thus began that strange mixed people, known as the Samaritans, who settled in the central part of the Holy Land.

The effect of Israel's doom upon the minds of the king and people of Judah may be imagined. From the pages of Micah and Isaiah, contemporary prophets in Judah, can be seen how God was speaking to Judah through the ruin of Israel. Ahaz's policy of relying on human help from Assyria instead of divine help from Jehovah was refuted by its outcome. With Syria and Samaria ruined, there lay nothing between Jerusalem and the Assyrian. And it is in Hezekiah's reign— the next after that of Ahaz—that the ruthless conqueror from Nineveh is found overrunning Judah itself. How king, prophet, and people met that crisis will begin the next lesson, for it belongs to the period when the Southern Kingdom is all that remained of the organized Hebrew nation in Palestine.

QUESTIONS ON LESSON X

1. What were the relations between the kingdoms of Judah and Israel in general?

2. Who altered these relations for a time? How? With what consequences for Judah's politics and religion?
3. Who was Joash, and how did he come to the throne?
4. What was the occasion of Judah's first intimate contact with Assyria? Discuss Ahaz's policy in the light of Isa. 7 : 1–9.
5. What were the stages in the downfall of the Northern Kingdom? What became of the conquered people, and who replaced them? See II Kings, ch. 17.

LESSON XI
Judah, from Hezekiah to the Exile

II Kings, Chapters 18 to 25 ; II Chronicles, Chapters 29 to 36; Isaiah (in part); Nahum; Habakkuk; Zephaniah; Jeremiah; Lamentations; Ezekiel, Chapters 1 to 32

Although outwardly Judah appeared to be the same after the fall of the Northern Kingdom as before, it was not so. A very different situation confronted Hezekiah from that which had confronted his father Ahaz when he called on Assyria for help against Syria and Israel. Now there were no "buffer states" between Assyria's empire and little Judah. And it was only a score of years after Samaria fell when Jerusalem felt the full force of Assyria. Sennacherib, fourth in that remarkable list of the six kings[1] who made Nineveh mistress of Asia, sent an army to besiege Jerusalem, with a summons to Hezekiah to surrender his capital.

A different spirit ruled this king. Isaiah, the same great prophet who had counseled Ahaz to resist Pekah and Rezin but had failed to move him to faith in Jehovah, found now in Ahaz's son a vital faith in the God of Israel in this far sorer crisis. In reponse to that faith Isaiah was commissioned by God to assure king and people of a great deliverance. The case, to all human seeming, was hopeless. But the resources at God's disposal are boundless, and at one blow "the angel of Jehovah" reduced the proud Assyrian host to impotency and drove them away in retreat. II Kings 19 : 35. Scribes who record the achievements of ancient monarchs are not accustomed to betray any of the failures of their royal heroes. But between the lines of Sennach-

---

[1] Tiglath-pileser, 745–727 B. c.; Shalmaneser, 727–722; Sargon, 722–705; Sennacherib, 705–681; Esar-haddon, 680–668; Ashurbanipal, 668–626.

erib's records we can read confirmation of the Bible's report of some great catastrophe to Assyrian arms. Jehovah rewarded the faith of his people in him.

The seventh century before Christ, which began just after this event, witnessed both the rise of Assyria to its greatest height, and its sudden fall before the Chaldeans, a people from the Persian Gulf, who succeeded in mastering ancient Babylon and in winning for it a greater glory than it had ever known in former times. Even in Hezekiah's reign these Chaldeans, under their leader Merodach-baladan, were already challenging the supremacy of Nineveh, and in doing so were seeking allies in the west. When the king of Judah yielded to the dictates of pride and showed to these Chaldean ambassadors his treasures, Isaiah announced to him that the final ruin of Judah was to come in future days from this source, and not from Nineveh as might then have been anticipated.

Manasseh, Hezekiah's successor, was indeed taken as a captive to Babylon for a time, but the captor was a king of Assyria. II Chron. 33 : 11. Manasseh was thus punished for his great personal wickedness, for he is pictured as the worst of all the descendants of David, an idolator and a cruel persecutor. Yet his reign was long, and at its close he is said to have repented and turned to Jehovah. But this did not prevent his son Amon from following in his evil ways. A revolt of the people within two years removed Amon, however, and set his young son, Josiah, upon the throne. Josiah's reign is important for the history of Judah.

By putting together all that can be gleaned from Kings, Chronicles, and the prophets, it can be seen that Josiah gradually came more and more under the influence of the party in Judah that sought to purge the nation of its idolatry and bring it back, not merely to the comparatively pure worship and life of Hezekiah's and David's days, but to an ideal observance of the ancient Law of Moses. The climax in the progressive reformation in Judah was reached in Josiah's eighteenth year, 622 B.C., when the king and all the people entered into a "solemn league and covenant" to obey the Law of Moses both as a religious obligation and as a social program.

The Law book which was found while workmen were restoring the Temple passed through the hands of Hilkiah, the high priest, who therefore committed himself, together with the priests, to this reform. And what the true prophets of Jehovah thought of it may be seen, for example, from Jer., ch. 11, which tells that this prophetic leader preached in the streets of Jerusalem and through the cities of Judah, saying, "Hear ye the words of this covenant, and do them."

Josiah attempted to attach to Jerusalem all those elements in the territory of the former kingdom of Israel which were in sympathy with Jehovah's Law, and at Bethel itself he defiled the old idolatrous altar and slew its priests. In fact, it was on northern ground, at Megiddo, that Josiah met his tragic end and the new wave of patriotic enthusiasm was shattered, when, in battle against Pharaoh-necho and a great Egyptian army, the king of Judah was killed.

Josiah's four successors were weak and unworthy of David's line. After Jehoahaz, the son whom the people put on the throne to succeed Josiah, had been removed by Necho, Jehoiakim, another son, reigned for eleven years. He owed his throne to the Pharaoh and was at first tributary to him. But early in his reign came the first of many campaigns of the Chaldeans into Palestine, as Nebuchadnezzar, master of Asia, extended his power farther and farther south after crushing the Egyptians at Carchemish in 605 B.C. Jehoiakim had to bow to Nebuchadnezzar's yoke and seems to have lost his life in a fruitless attempt to shake it off. A great number of the leaders of Judah, nobles, priests, soldiers, and craftsmen, were deported, together with Jehoiachin, the young son of Jehoiakim, who had worn the crown but three months, 598 B.C.

For eleven years more, however, the remnant of Judah maintained a feeble state under Zedekiah, a third son of Josiah and the last of David's line to mount the throne. In spite of his solemn oath to the king of Babylon and in the face of the express warnings from Jehovah through his prophets Jeremiah and Ezekiel, this weak and faithless king revolted from Babylon, put his trust in the Egyptian army, and prepared to stand a siege. But Jerusalem's end had now come, as Samaria's had come before, and through a breach in the northern wall the Chaldean army entered; the king fled and was captured, blinded, and deported, and the whole city, including houses, walls, gates, and even the Temple—that famous Temple of Solomon which had stood nearly four centuries—was totally destroyed, 587 B.C. All that remained of the higher classes, together with the population of Jerusalem and the chief towns, were carried away to Babylonia, to begin that exile which had been threatened even in the Law, and predicted by many of the prophets, as the extreme penalty for disobedience and idolatry.

QUESTIONS ON LESSON XI

1. How did the fall of Samaria affect the Kingdom of Judah?
2. How did Hezekiah meet the threats of Sennacherib? What was the outcome?
3. Which king carried through a reformation of religion? What was the basis of the covenant he imposed on Judah? How did he meet his end?
4. Describe the relations of the Chaldeans to Judah in the time of Hezekiah, of Jehoiakim, of Zedekiah?
5. When did Jerusalem fall? Did it fall unexpectedly and without warning?

LESSON XII
The Exile and the Restoration

Ezekiel, Chapters 33 to 48; Daniel; Ezra, Chapters 1, 2

When the northern tribes were carried away by Assyria they lost their identity in the mass of the nations. Only individuals from among them attached themselves to the organized nucleus of Judah. From that time the one tribe of Judah stood out so prominently as representative of the whole nation, that "Jew" (that is, man of Judah) has been equivalent to Hebrew. Paul says that he was of the tribe of Benjamin; the aged prophetess Anna is said to have been of the tribe of Asher, Luke 2 : 36, and all the priests were of course of the tribe of Levi; yet long before New Testament times all such Israelites were commonly referred to as "Jews."

Judah did not lose its identity among the nations when Jerusalem fell. The Jews who were not deported, among them the prophet Jeremiah, were put under the government of a certain Jewish noble, Gedaliah, who ruled the land from Mizpah as representative of the great king. Many fugitives returned to live under his sway when they found that it was beneficent. But Gedaliah was soon murdered by a prince of David's house, whom the king of Ammon had set on to do this mischief and then received and protected. The other Jewish leaders feared to remain within reach of the king of Babylon after this insult to him, and against the warnings of Jeremiah they all went down to Egypt. That removal ended all organized Jewish life in Palestine for nearly half a century.

In Babylon, however, an event occurred long before that time had elapsed, which marked the political recognition of Judah's separate identity as a nation. That event was the release of Jehoiachin from prison by the new king of Babylon, Evil-merodach, successor of Nebuchadnezzar. Jehoiachin, it will be remembered, was the unfortunate prince of David's line who held the throne only three months after his father Jehoiakim's death and was then deported to Babylon in 598. From that time on, through all the remainder of Nebuchadnezzar's long reign, he had been imprisoned in Babylon. But now he was not only released, but given a pension from the royal treasury for the rest of his life and a standing superior to all the other captive princes in Babylon.

This was in 562, and many Jewish hearts must already have begun to beat with fresh hope, as the old loyalty to David's house flamed up, and the promises of a restoration recorded in the old Law and the Prophets were echoed by the prophet of the Exile, Ezekiel. This man, himself a priest by birth, had been carried to Babylon at the same time as Jehoiachin, and through all those years of doom had there preached to his countrymen, first to the portion exiled with him while Jerusalem still stood, but after 587 to the whole people united in a common catastrophe. His voice had even reached to Jerusalem, as he joined Jeremiah in reminding King Zedekiah of his oath to Nebuchadnezzar. With the elevation of Jehoiachin and the stirring of the national hopes, Ezekiel became the prophet of hope. He pictures the breath of Jehovah stirring to life the dry bones in the valley of death. Ezek., ch. 37. And he warns the optimistic people that only as God takes away from them their old stony heart and gives them a heart of flesh, and sprinkles clean water upon them to cleanse them from their pollution through idolatry, can they be fit to form the new community wherein God shall indeed reign. Ch. 36 : 25, 26. What such a community might outwardly and visibly resemble, Ezekiel pictures in a long, detailed, descriptive vision wherewith his book closes. Chs. 40 to 48.

Another outstanding Jew of the Exile was a man of an entirely different type. Daniel, a noble youth carried away from Judah to Babylon at the first clash of Nebuchadnezzar's armies with the Jews, 605 B.C., and brought up at the court, succeeded through interpreting a dream of the king in attracting his notice and winning his favor, much as Joseph had done in ancient Egypt. Dan., ch. 2. From his position of political power, Daniel was able, doubtless, to minister to the interests of his brethren, the Jewish exiles. Possibly it is to him that Jehoiachin owed his astonishing reversal of fortune. At any rate Belshazzar, the last ruler of the Chaldean state, still maintained Daniel in power, in spite of the very solemn warning of ruin to that state which Daniel fearlessly pronounced. Ch. 5. When the Persians succeeded the Chaldeans as masters of Babylon, this Jewish statesman still held his high post, and retained it in spite of the bitter enmity of officials who used his Jewish faith as a handle against him. Ch. 6. In fact, there is no better way to understand the favor accorded the Jews by Cyrus, the Persian conqueror, and the edicts preserved in Ezra 1 : 2–4; 6 : 3–5, than by supposing that Daniel, who had the king's ear, brought to his attention the earlier prophecies of Jeremiah and of other spokesmen for Jehovah, God of the Jews.

Certainly, however the affair was managed, it turned out entirely to the Jews' liking. All who were willing to return to Palestine were permitted and encouraged to go. They were assisted by the gifts of their brethren who could not, or would not, leave Babylon. They bore back with them the old vessels for the service of the sanctuary which Nebuchadnezzar had carried off. And, best of all, they took with them royal authority to erect the Temple of Jehovah on its ancient site, at the expense of the king of Persia, that is, out of taxes and tribute he remitted. At their head went a prince of the old royal house, and a high priest who was grandson of that high priest whom Nebuchadnezzar had executed half a century before. Their number totaled forty-two thousand three hundred and sixty, with enough slaves in addition to make the entire company number nearly fifty thousand.

Their purpose was threefold: to reoccupy the Holy Land, to rebuild Jerusalem, and to erect a temple where Solomon's Temple had stood. We should be likely to rate the importance of these three objects in the same order as that in which they have just been named. But not so the believing Jew. It was above all else the sacred house of his God that he wanted to see restored, so that the prescribed sacrifices of the Law might be resumed, the nation's sin might thus be atoned for, and God might once more visibly dwell among his people. All else was in order to this one great end. The origin of Judaism, which lies in the movements of this time, cannot be understood unless this supreme motive is clearly grasped. How Judaism developed under the new conditions will be the subject of the next lesson.

QUESTIONS ON LESSON XII

1. What is meant by "a Jew"?
2. How did government of Hebrews by a Hebrew come to an end in Palestine for the first time since Saul's day?
3. What was the first political event to arouse the exiled Jews from their depression?
4. Compare Ezekiel and Daniel in their personality, position, and audience.
5. When Cyrus captured Babylon in 539, what did he do for the Jews, and how came he to do it?
6. How many Jews returned to Palestine under Cyrus, and what was their uppermost motive?

LESSON XIII

The Jewish State Under Persia

Ezra, Chapters 3 to 10; Esther; Nehemiah; Haggai; Zechariah; Malachi

For two centuries Judea, like the rest of western Asia, was under the domination of the Persians, whose great royal names, Cyrus, Darius, Xerxes, Artaxerxes, are familiar to every student of history. The Old Testament spans one of those two centuries of Persian rule, 539–430, while for the other century, 430–332, we are dependent for the little we know about the Jews upon some documents recently discovered in Egypt, an occasional notice in classical historians, and the brief narrative of Josephus, the Jewish historian of the first Christian century.

Even in the century covered by the books of the Bible there are long stretches of silence separating periods that are fairly reported. First comes the time of Zerubbabel and Jeshua, the leaders, civil and religious, under whom the Jews returned and erected the Temple. This story carries us, though with a seventeen-year gap in its midst, from 538, the year after Cyrus took Babylon, to 515, the sixth year of Darius the Great, and is recorded in the first six chapters of the book of Ezra. To help us in understanding this time we have also the prophecies of Haggai and Zechariah, though the last six chapters of Zechariah belong to another age.

After the completion of the new Temple the curtain falls on Judea and, save for a single verse, Ezra 4 : 6, we hear no more of it for fifty-seven years. However, the interesting story of Esther belongs in these years, for the Ahasuerus of the Bible is the Xerxes of Greek history—that vain, fickle, and voluptuous monarch who was beaten at Salamis and Platæa. The Jews must have been a part of the vast host with which he crossed from Asia to Europe. But the drama unfolded in the book of Esther was played far from Palestine, at Susa, the Persian capital.

With the seventh year of the next reign—that of Artaxerxes I—the curtain rises again on Judea, as we accompany thither the little band of Jews whom Ezra, the priestly "scribe," brought back with him from Babylonia to Jerusalem. This account is found in the last four chapters of the book of Ezra, most of it in the form of personal reminiscences covering less than one year.

The curtain falls again abruptly at the end of Ezra's memoirs, and rises as abruptly on Nehemiah's memoirs at the beginning of the book which bears his name. But there is every reason to believe that the letters exchanged between the Samaritans and the Persian court, preserved in the fourth chapter of Ezra, belong to this interval of thirteen years between the two books of Ezra and Nehemiah. For this alone can explain two riddles: first, who are "the men that came up from thee unto Jerusalem," Ezra 4 : 12, if they are not Ezra and his company, ch. 7? And second, what else could explain the desolate condition of Jerusalem and Nehemiah's emotion on learning of it, Neh. 1 : 3, if not the mischief wrought by the Jews' enemies when "they went in haste to Jerusalem," armed with a royal injunction, and "made them to cease by force and power"? Ezra 4 : 23.

Some persons are inclined to date the prophet Malachi at just this time also, shortly before Nehemiah's arrival. But it is probably better to place the ministry of this last of the Old Testament prophets at the end of Nehemiah's administration. Nehemiah's points of contact with Malachi are most numerous in his last chapter, ch. 13, in which he writes of his later visit to Jerusalem. Compare Neh. 13 : 6 with ch. 1 : 1.

In Cyrus' reign the great Return was followed immediately by the erection of an altar and the resumption of sacrifice. Preparations for rebuilding the Temple, however, and even the laying of the corner stone, proved a vain beginning, as the Samaritans, jealous of the newcomers and angered by their own rebuff as fellow worshipers with the Jews, succeeded in hindering the prosecution of the work for many years. Ezra 3 : 1 to 4 : 5.

It was not until the second year of Darius' reign, 520, nearly two decades later, that the little community, spurred out of their selfishness and lethargy by Haggai and Zechariah, arose and completed the new Temple, in the face of local opposition but with royal support. Ch. 4 : 24 to 6 : 15.

Fifty-seven years later, in the seventh year of Artaxerxes, 458, came Ezra with some fifteen hundred men, large treasures, and sweeping privileges confirmed by a royal edict, the text of which he has preserved in the seventh chapter of his book. He was given the king's support in introducing the Law of God as the law of the land, binding upon all its inhabitants, whom he was to teach its contents and punish for infractions of it. How Ezra used his exceptional powers in carrying out the reform he judged most needed—the dissolution of mixed marriages between Jew and Gentile forbidden by the Law—is told in detail in his own vivid language in chs. 9, 10. It helps us to understand Malachi's zeal in this same matter. Mal. 2 : 11. And the difficulty of this reform appears also from Nehemiah's memoirs, since the same abuse persisted twenty-five years after Ezra fought it. Neh. 13 : 23–27.

After the failure to fortify Jerusalem recorded in Ezra 4 : 8–23, Nehemiah, a Jew in high station and favor at Artaxerxes' court, obtained from his king a personal letter, appointing him governor of Judea for a limited time, with the special commission to rebuild the walls and gates of Jerusalem. The same bitter hostility which the Samaritans and other neighbors in Palestine throughout had shown toward the returned Jews, reached its climax in the efforts of Sanballat and others in public and private station to hinder Nehemiah's purpose. But with great energy and bravery, and with a personal appeal and example that swept all into the common stream of patriotic service, Nehemiah built the ruined walls and gates in fifty-two days, instituted social reforms, ch. 5, and imposed a covenant on all the people to obey the Law which Ezra read and expounded. Chs. 8 to 10. Elements in the little nation that joined with his enemies to discredit and even to assassinate him were banished or curbed. The origin of the peculiar sect of the Samaritan is connected with Nehemiah through his rigor in banishing a grandson of the high priest who had married Sanballat's daughter. This disloyalty of the priesthood is also one of Malachi's chief indictments against his nation, and the basis of his promise that a great reformer, an "Elijah," should arise to prepare the sinful people for the coming of their God.

QUESTIONS ON LESSON XIII

1. How long after the Return was the Temple finished? Who hindered? Who helped?
2. What are the scene and the date of the book of Esther?
3. Compare the return of the Jews to Jerusalem under Ezra with that under Zerubbabel (*a*) in date, (*b*) in numbers, (*c*) in purpose and result.
4. Tell the story of Nehemiah: the occasion of his return, his enemies, his achievements. In what did Ezra help him?
5. Associate the ministry of the three prophets of this period after the Exile with the leaders and movements they respectively helped.

LESSON XIV
Israel's Religious Life

It has often been said that while civilization owes its art and letters to Greece and its law and order to Rome, it owes its religion and ethics to Palestine. This is true, within limits, provided we understand that what Israel contributed was not the product of its "native genius for religion," but was due to the persistent grace of its God, who took this "fewest of all peoples" and made of it the custodian of his revelation and the cradle of his redemption for the whole world. When, however, the Hebrew claimed preëminence through these two things, a saving God and a righteous Law, it was no idle boast. So Moses eloquently asks in Deuteronomy: "What great nation is there, that hath a god so nigh unto them, as Jehovah our God is whensoever we call upon him? And what great nation is there, that hath statutes and ordinances so righteous as all this law, which I set before you this day?" Deut. 4 : 7, 8.

Religion as developed in Israel had two sides, an inward and an outward. On its inward side it consisted of a faith in Jehovah cherished in the hearts of the people, together with the sentiments of reverence and love, and the purposes of loyalty and consecration, which grew out of that faith. On its outward side religion consisted of certain objects and ceremonies, adapted to express by act and symbol the relation between God and his people.

But there is also another distinction often made in speaking of religion, the distinction between individual religion and national religion. Each member of the Hebrew nation held a personal relation to his God. The Law of God addressed him individually as it said to him, "Thou shalt not." And, on a still higher level, Moses summed up that Law for him in these memorable words, "Thou shalt love the Lord thy God with all thy heart." Yet the entire body of Israel, as such, held a relation to God which his spokesmen are continually trying to illustrate and enrich by all sorts of figures. God is Israel's "Rock," "Possessor" or "Purchaser," "Redeemer," "Father"—until Isaiah can even say to the nation, "Thy Maker is thy husband," and Hosea and Ezekiel can portray God's dealings with Israel under the allegory of a marriage.

It would be a mistake, however, to suppose that all the inward religion was individual and all the outward religion national. There was provision in the ceremonial law, not only for sacrifices on a national scale, like those of the day of atonement, but also for each man to express outwardly his own penitence or devotion or gratitude or obligation to God by means of a personal sacrifice, publicly offered but privately planned and provided. And, on the other hand, the psalms and the prophets cannot be understood, unless we realize the general religious life of the nation that lies back of these highly individual forms of expression. That was why, when David thinking of himself could write, "The Lord is my shepherd," the whole people could take that sentence and the psalm it begins for use in public worship as the collective expression of Israel's trust in its God.

The great fact of sin is responsible for the perversion of the true relation between these different varieties of religious life. In theory, every symbolic object and action at tabernacle or Temple was merely the outward expression of an inward idea or feeling or resolve. Every smoking sacrifice on the altar was supposed to come from an offerer drawing near to God in the sincere belief "that he is, and that he is a rewarder of them that seek after him." Heb. 11 : 6. But in fact the offerer was in constant danger of looking upon all the gifts and victims he brought as so many bribes with which he might buy the favor of an offended God, or, worse still, might obtain an "indulgence" to do some evil deed he planned. This is what Jeremiah means when he cries, "Will ye steal, murder, and commit adultery, and swear falsely . . . and come and stand before me in this house, which is called by my name, and say, We are delivered; that ye may do all these abominations?" Jer. 7 : 9, 10.

If the private worshiper was in danger of abusing the worship of God in this way, how much more was the priest, the professional sacrificer and celebrant, in danger of looking upon all his duties as a kind of authorized magic! "Do this external act, and that inward benefit will surely follow." "Offer this lamb, and cease to think about that black sin for which the lamb is the official price." Yes, even this: "Go and do it again, but don't forget to bring another lamb!" Is it any wonder that at length Malachi, after lashing the priests of his late day for their laziness, cynicism, and greed, cries out in Jehovah's name, "Oh that there were one among you that would shut the doors [of the Temple], that ye might not kindle fire on mine altar in vain!" Mal. 1 : 10.

All along the course of Hebrew history we find prophets and psalmists protesting against this sinful perversion of ceremonial religion. See for example I Sam. 15 : 22; Ps. 40 : 6–8; 50; Isa. 1 : 10–17; Micah 6 : 6–8.

And yet it would be a mistake to say that the prophet stood for pure and spiritual religion, and the priest for merely external, formal religion. Some of the greatest of the prophets, as Jeremiah, Ezekiel, Zechariah, were priests. And how far the prophets could become professional declaimers and deceivers may be seen, for example, from Micah 3 : 5–8.

The Hebrew prophets, notably Amos and Hosea, are sometimes represented as the "inventors" of "ethical monotheism," that is, of religion as consisting in the worship of one God, who is the moral ideal of man and demands moral living in man. But in fact, that is precisely the basis of all genuine Old Testament religion, from the very beginning. See Heb., ch. 11. And, particularly, that is the basis of the entire Law, even of the ceremonial law. For that Law must not be judged by its sinful abuse, but by the principles of righteousness, holiness, repentance, and fellowship that underlie every article in the sanctuary, every sacrifice on the altar, every rite prescribed and observance commanded. At their best the priests were allies of the true prophets, and external religion as centering in the Temple was for the time a fitting expression of Israel's personal and national faith. If it had not been so, then such psalms as Psalms 24, 42, 65, 84, 122 could never have been written, preserved, and used.

QUESTIONS ON LESSON XIV

1. What ground had Israel for "glorying"? See Rom. 9 : 4, 5.
2. Give illustrations to show that individual as well as national religion in Israel expressed itself externally, and that spiritual as

well as ceremonial religion belonged to both the nation and the individual.

3. What sinful abuse of sacrifice were the prophets constantly attacking? Did they thereby condemn Temple, altar, priesthood, and ceremonial law in themselves?

4. Were all the prophets spiritually minded, or all the priests merely "professional"? Give instances from history of alliances between prophets and priests.

LESSON XV
"The Coming One"

The Old Testament points forward. The whole impression it leaves upon us is that of an unfinished thing. Its history moves toward a goal outside of itself. Its religion is a religion of expectation. All its institutions are typical, that is, they represent more than themselves, because they belong to a larger order of things which appears imperfectly in them.

In the last lesson we saw how priest and prophet had their own place in Israel. But both priest and prophet also typified a perfect priesthood and a perfect prophecy, to be realized under ideal conditions which were never present in those times. When, for example, Aaron made atonement for the sins of the nation once each year, as provided in Lev., ch. 16, he had to present first the blood of the bullock which was the sin offering for himself, before he presented the blood of the goat which was the sin offering for the people. But ideally, in his position as mediator between God and the sinful people, he was a sinless man; the blood of the bullock and the pure, white garments he put on were supposed to indicate that he was sinless for the moment. Nothing could be clearer than that he typified a perfect high priest for God's people, who should be really a sinless man—one who needed no mechanism of altar, victim, and dress to make him pure from personal sin. See Heb., chs. 5 to 10, especially ch. 7 : 26–28.

Again Moses looks forward to the realization in the future of the ideal communication between God and his people typified in the prophet. "A prophet," says he, "Jehovah thy God will raise up unto thee." "From the midst of thee, like unto me." Deut. 18 : 15–19. This ideal prophet will perfectly hear and perfectly transmit divine truth to men. It was on the basis of this promise that many persons described our Lord as "the prophet," meaning thereby that perfect prophet promised by Moses. John 1 : 21, 25; 7 : 40.

But there was another institution of Old Testament times which more than prophet or priest was associated in the people's minds with the ideal future. This was kingship. God himself was theoretically King—sole King—of Israel. Isa. 33 : 22. But at the entreaty of his sinful and harassed people he instructed Samuel to "make them a king." And while Samuel warned them of the evils which the monarchy would bring with it because of the sinfulness of the men who should be king, he nevertheless set up a throne that by its very nature was unique. The king of Israel was in a peculiar sense the representative of Jehovah. He ruled for God. He was his own "anointed," set apart for the exercise of supreme authority over God's people on earth and entitled to their religious as well as patriotic devotion. See, for example, Psalms 21, 101.

After the failure of Saul to obey God's instructions, Samuel anointed, at God's dictation and against his own human judgment, David the son of Jesse. This man proved himself, not indeed sinless nor the ideal king, but a man after God's heart, Acts 13 : 22, because his dominant purpose was to do God's will. To David therefore was given the remarkable promise contained in II Sam., ch. 7. In a word, this promise was an irrevocable, eternal "covenant," granting sovereignty to David's "house"—that is, his posterity considered as a unit—over God's Kingdom on earth.

The story of how men came to understand better and better the vastness of this covenant, which Isaiah calls "the sure mercies of David," ch. 55 : 3, forms the subject of that special Old Testament study called "Messianic Prophecy." In the psalms and in the prophecies we are able to trace a growing faith, that by an ideal king of David's line Jehovah will finally work his long delayed will in and through Israel. This Person is commonly called "the Messiah," because "Messiah" means "Anointed." Its Greek equivalent is "the Christ." While other persons also were anointed with oil when they assumed office, kings were always so anointed and the idea belongs peculiarly to kingship. By the time our Lord appeared, no other side of the work which this ideal, promised, longed-for Coming One was to do, was so prominent as that of ruling for God as the King of Israel. For this reason Jesus of Nazareth is known to all who believe in his claims as "the Christ," and such believers are thence called "Christians." This title of Christ connects Jesus with the line of David, to which he actually belonged by descent, and it also connects him with the promise to David, of which he was the heir and the fulfillment.

We have thus seen that "the Coming One," Luke 7 : 19; John 11 : 27, toward whom the eyes of Israel were directed, was to be prophet, priest, and king. In all these offices and the various duties they involved he was to be the one chosen from among the people—a man therefore, "servant of the servants of God." Yet this is not all. Alongside these promises there was a promise also that Jehovah himself would come to dwell among his people. The Holy of Holies, with its Ark of the Presence and its Mercy seat for revelation and atonement, was itself typical of an ideal presence of God among men. And through psalm and prophet we can trace this promise also. Now it is terrible with its threat to sinners, and now it is glorious with its hope for the oppressed. At length in Malachi we read in the clearest words, "The Lord, whom ye seek, will suddenly come to his temple." Mal. 3 : 1, 5. Preceded by his "messenger" to "prepare the way before him," Israel's divine Lord himself is to come for judgment and salvation. See also Ps. 96 : 13; 98 : 9.

It was not made so plain to the men of ancient Israel just how these two lines of promise were to be united, as it appears to us now in the light of later facts. But we, who worship Jesus of Nazareth not only as "Son of David according to the flesh," but as divine Lord from heaven, "in two distinct natures and one person for ever," can look back on those old prophecies of "men who spake from God, being moved by the Holy Spirit." II Peter 1 : 21. We can see in them God's purpose to make this great Son of David a true "Immanuel," Isa. 7 : 14—a Person in whom God actually is "with us." God gave to him such names as "Wonderful, Counsellor, Mighty God, Everlasting Father, Prince of Peace," because he should really be all that these names imply. Isa. 9 : 6. For the Child who was born in little Bethlehem, the "city of David," was not merely one who should be "ruler in Israel," but also one "whose goings forth are from of old, from everlasting." Micah 5 : 2.

QUESTIONS ON LESSON XV

1. How did the priests and prophets in Israel point forward to an ideal Priest and Prophet?

2. What was the relation of Israel's king to Jehovah? In whose "house" was this office made eternal? In what Person has this promise been fulfilled?

3. How was the promise that God himself should be "the Coming One" consistent with the promise of a human Prophet, Priest, and King? Where is it indicated in the Old Testament that both promises might be fulfilled in one Person?

SECTION II

The Life of Christ and the Development of the Church in New Testament Times

By John Gresham Machen, D.D.

LESSON I

The Preparation

At the time when the Old Testament narrative closes, the Jews were under the rule of Persia. The Persian control continued for about one hundred years more, and then gave way to the empire of Alexander the Great. Alexander was king of Macedonia, a country to the north of Greece; but the language and culture of his court were Greek. After Greece proper had been conquered by Alexander's father, Philip, Alexander himself proceeded to the conquest of the East. The Persian Empire fell in 331 B.C., and with the other Persian possessions Jerusalem came into the hands of the conqueror. In 323 B.C., when Alexander died, his vast empire, which extended around the eastern end of the Mediterranean Sea and to the borders of India, at once fell to pieces. But the kingdoms into which the empire was divided were to a large extent Greek kingdoms. Short-lived, therefore, as Alexander's empire was, it had the permanent effect of spreading the Greek language and Greek civilization over the Eastern world. It became thus, as will be seen, one of the most important factors in the divine preparation for the gospel.

After the death of Alexander, the country of Judea became a bone of contention between two of the kingdoms into which Alexander's empire was divided—the Greek kingdom of Syria and the Greek kingdom of Egypt. At last, however, the Syrian kingdom, with its capital at Antioch, near the northeastern corner of the Mediterranean Sea, gained the upper hand. Judea became part of the territory of the Syrian monarchs.

In the reign of Antiochus IV of Syria, called Antiochus Epiphanes, 175–164 B.C., the Jews began a war for independence. Antiochus Epiphanes had desecrated the Temple at Jerusalem by setting up an image of a heathen god in the Holy of Holies. The result was the glorious revolt of the Jews under Mattathias and his sons—the family of the Maccabees. The Maccabean uprising, of which a stirring account has been preserved in the First Book of the Maccabees, an apocryphal book attached to the Old Testament, certainly constitutes one of the most glorious chapters in the history of liberty. The uprising was successful, and for about one hundred years the little country of the

55

Jews, though surrounded by powerful neighbors, succeeded in maintaining its independence.

At first the Maccabees had been animated by a religious motive; the revolt had been due not to an interference with what may be called civil liberty, but to the desecration by Antiochus Epiphanes of the Temple and to the attempt at prohibiting the worship of Jehovah. As time went on, however, the Maccabean rulers became more worldly in their purposes and thus alienated the devout element among their people. Hence the little kingdom became an easy prey to the next great world empire which appeared upon the scene.

That empire was the empire of Rome. Originally a small city-state in Italy, Rome had gradually extended her conquests until she came into conflict with Greece and with the Greek kingdoms of the Eastern world. Weakened by many causes, the successors of Alexander soon succumbed, and among them the monarchs of Syria. Judea could not resist the new conqueror. In 63 B.C., the famous Roman general, Pompey, entered Jerusalem, and Jewish independence was at an end.

The Roman control was exerted in Palestine for a time through subservient high priests, until in 37 B.C. Herod the Great was made king. Herod was not a real Jew, but an Idumæan; and at heart he had little or no attachment to the Jews' religion. But he was wise enough not to offend Jewish feeling in the outrageous way that had proved so disastrous to Antiochus Epiphanes. Throughout his reign Herod was of course thoroughly subservient to the Romans; though a king, he was strictly a vassal king. Herod reigned from 37 B.C. to 4 B.C. His kingdom embraced not only Judea, but all Palestine. It was near the end of Herod's reign that our Saviour was born. Thus the reckoning of the Christian era, which was instituted many centuries after Christ, is at least four years too low; Jesus was born a little earlier than 4 B.C.

When Pompey conquered Jerusalem in 63 B.C., Rome was still a republic. But before many years had elapsed Julius Cæsar assumed the supreme power, and the ancient Roman liberties were gone. After the assassination of Cæsar in 44 B.C., there was a long period of civil war. Finally Augustus was triumphant, and the Roman Empire began. In the long reign of Augustus, 27 B.C. to A.D. 14, our Saviour was born.

The political events which have just been outlined did not take place by chance. They were all parts of the plan of God which prepared for the coming of the Lord. When Jesus finally came, the world was prepared for his coming.

In the first place, the Roman Empire provided that peace and unity which was needed for the spread of the gospel. War interrupts communication between nations. But when the apostles went forth from Jerusalem to spread the good news of Christ to the world, there was no war to interrupt their course. Nation was bound to nation under the strong hand of Rome. Travel was comparatively safe and easy, and despite occasional persecution the earliest missionaries usually enjoyed the protection of Roman law.

In the second place, the Greek language provided a medium of communication. When the Romans conquered the Eastern world, they did not endeavor to substitute their own language for the language which already prevailed. Such an attempt would only have produced confusion. Indeed, the Romans themselves adopted the Greek language as a convenient medium of communication. Greek thus became a world language. The original, local languages of the various countries continued to be used (Aramaic, for example, was used in Palestine), but Greek was a common medium. Thus when the apostles went forth to the evangelization of the world, there were no barriers of language to check their course.

In the third place, the dispersion of the Jews provided the early missionaries everywhere with a starting point for their labors. As a result not only of captivity, but also of voluntary emigration, the Jews in the first century were scattered abroad throughout the cities of the world very much as they are scattered to-day. But there was one important difference. To-day the Jewish synagogues are attended only by Jews. In those days they were attended also by men of other races. Thus when Paul and the other Christian missionaries exercised their privilege of speaking in the synagogues, they were speaking not only to Jews but also to a picked audience of Gentiles.

QUESTIONS ON LESSON I

1. Name in order the foreign powers which possessed the country of the Jews, beginning with Old Testament times and continuing down to the present day.
2. What was the importance of the Maccabean uprising in the preparation for the coming of the Lord? What would have happened if Antiochus Epiphanes had been successful?
3. What was the importance of the Roman Empire for the spread of the gospel? of the Greek language? of the dispersion of the Jews?

LESSON II
The Coming of the Lord
John 1: 1-18

When the Son of God came to earth for our salvation, the world was ready for his coming. The whole course of history had been made to lead up to him. And he was well worthy of being thus the goal of history. For the One who came was none other than the eternal Son of God, the Word who was with God and who was God. He had existed from all eternity; he had been the instrument in creating the world. He was himself truly God, the same in substance with the Father, and equal in power and glory. Yet the One who was so great humbled himself to be born as a man and finally to suffer and die. His coming was a voluntary act, an act of the Father in giving him for the sins of the world, and his own act which he performed because he loved us. It was an act of infinite condescension. The Son of God humbled himself to lead a true human life; he took upon himself our nature. He was born, he grew in wisdom and stature, he suffered, he died. He was always God, but he became also man. Who can measure the depth of such condescending love?

What, then, was the manner of his coming? The story is told, in beautiful narrative, in the first two chapters of Matthew and Luke.

Luke 1: 5-25, 57-80

First, the birth of John the Baptist, the forerunner, was announced by the angel Gabriel to Zacharias, a devout priest, as he was ministering in the Temple. Luke 1 : 5–25. Zacharias was old; he had given up hope of children. The promise seemed to him too wonderful to be true; he doubted the angel's word. But the punishment which was inflicted upon him for his doubt was temporary merely, and the bitterness of it was swallowed up in joy for the child that was born. The tongue of Zacharias, which had been dumb on account of his sin, was loosed, and he uttered a wonderful song of praise. Vs. 57–80.

Luke 1: 26-56

But before John was born, in fulfillment of the angel's promise, there was a promise of a greater than John. Luke 1 : 26–56. "The angel Gabriel was sent from God unto a city of Galilee, named Nazareth, to a virgin betrothed to a man whose name was Joseph, of the house of David; and the virgin's name was Mary." It was a far more wonderful promise than that which had come to Zacharias, not only because of the greater glory of the promised Son, but also because of the mystery of his birth. The child was to have no human father, but was to be given by the power of the Holy Spirit. But this time, despite the strangeness of the promise, there was no unbelief, as in the case of Zacharias. "Behold, the handmaid of the Lord," said Mary; "be it unto me according to thy word." And then Mary went to Judea to visit her kinswoman Elisabeth, the wife of Zacharias; and while in Judea she gave glorious expression to her thanksgiving in the hymn which is called, from the first word of it in the Latin translation, the "Magnificat"— "My soul doth magnify the Lord, and my spirit hath rejoiced in God my Saviour." Then Mary returned to her own home in Nazareth.

Matthew 1:18-25

But another announcement of the Saviour's birth was made to Joseph, who was betrothed to Mary. Matt. 1 : 18–25. Joseph was to have the high privilege of caring for the child that was to be born. "Fear not to take unto thee Mary thy wife," said the angel to Joseph in a dream, "for that which is conceived in her is of the Holy Spirit." And here again, there was no unbelief and no disobedience. Joseph "did as the angel of the Lord commanded him, and took unto him his wife."

Luke 2:1-7

Joseph and Mary lived in Nazareth, a town of the northern part of Palestine, which was called Galilee. But the promised Child was to belong to the house of David, and it was fitting that he should be born at Bethlehem, a little town five miles south of Jerusalem where David himself had been born. To cause him to be born at Bethlehem, God made use of an event of world politics. Luke 2 : 1–7. A decree had gone out from the emperor, Augustus, that the whole empire should be enrolled. This enrollment or census seems to have been carried out in the kingdom of Herod the Great by the Jewish method which took account of family relationships. So, although at the time Joseph and Mary were living at Nazareth, they went up to the home of Joseph's ancestors, to Bethlehem, to be enrolled. And at Bethlehem the Saviour was born. There was no room in the lodging place. The Child was laid, therefore, in a manger that was intended for the feeding of cattle.

Luke 2: 8-20

But humble as were the surroundings of the newborn King, his birth was not without manifestations of glory. Luke 2 : 8–20. Shepherds, keeping watch in the fields by night, heard a multitude of the heavenly host praising God and saying, "Glory to God in the highest, and on earth peace among men in whom he is well pleased." The shepherds went then to see the sign which had been made known to them. It was a strange sign indeed—Christ the Lord, the promised King, wrapped in swaddling clothes and lying in a manger!

Luke 2: 21-38; Matthew 2: 1-12

Forty days after the birth of Jesus, Joseph and Mary made the offering according to the Old Testament law, and presented the Child, as the first-born, to the Lord in the Temple at Jerusalem. Luke 2 : 21–38. Then they must have returned to Bethlehem, for it was at Bethlehem that gifts were presented by Wise Men from the East. Matt. 2 : 1–12. The Wise Men had been guided to Bethlehem partly by a wonderful star which they had first seen in their own country, and partly by questions which were answered by the scribes.

Matthew 2: 13-23

But the life of the infant Saviour was not all to be a hearing of angels' songs and a reception of gold and frankincense and myrrh. The Lord had come to suffer for the sins of the world, and the last great suffering on the cross was anticipated by the persecution which came in the early days. Matt. 2 : 13–18. The suspicions of Herod, the jealous king, had been aroused by the questions of the Wise Men. He sent to Bethlehem to put a possible rival out of the way. But it was too late. The king's rage was vented upon the innocent children of the little town, but God had cared for the infant Saviour. The Lord was finally to die for the sins of the world. But meanwhile many words of wisdom and grace were to fall from his lips; his hour was not yet come. Joseph was warned of God in a dream, and took the young Child and his mother away to Egypt, out of the way of harm, until Herod the Great was dead. Then they returned to Nazareth, where the Child was to spend long, quiet years of preparation for his work.

QUESTIONS ON LESSON II

1. What life had our Saviour lived before he came to earth? Did he cease to be God while he was on earth?
2. Why did he come?
3. Who was his forerunner? What sort of persons were the parents of the forerunner?
4. How did Jesus come to be born at Bethlehem?
5. What was the character of his mother?

LESSON III

The Baptism

Luke 2: 40-50

The New Testament tells very little about the boyhood and early manhood of our Saviour. One incident, however, is narrated. Luke 2 : 41–50. Joseph and Mary, we are told, were in the habit of going up from Galilee to Jerusalem every year in the spring at the feast of the passover. When Jesus was twelve years old, he went up with them. But when they left Jerusalem on the return, Jesus remained behind in the Temple, to study the Old Testament; and when Joseph and Mary found him, he replied to their inquiries, "Knew ye not that I must be about my Father's business?" The incident shows the presence even in the human consciousness of the boy Jesus of a knowledge of the great mission that he was called to fulfill and of his special relation to God.

Luke 2: 51, 52

But the consciousness of these great things did not prevent our Saviour from performing the humble tasks of daily life and from being obedient to his human parents. Luke 2 : 51, 52. Jesus became a carpenter, and since Joseph also was a carpenter, no doubt Jesus learned the trade in early youth. Mark 6 : 3; Matt. 13 : 55. For many years, till he was about thirty years old, the Saviour of the world labored at the carpenter's bench, and lived as an obedient son in a humble home at Nazareth. Luke 3 : 23.

At last, however, the time came for the beginning of his public ministry. Before that ministry is studied, it may be well to cast a glance at the condition of the country into which Jesus now came forward.

When Herod the Great died in 4 B.C., his dominions were divided among his three sons. Archelaus received Judea, the southern part of Palestine, with Jerusalem as its chief city; Herod Antipas, the "Herod" who is mentioned in the Gospels in connection with Jesus' public ministry, received Galilee and a district to the east of the Jordan River called Perea; and Philip received a region lying to the east of Galilee and to the north of Perea. When Archelaus was banished in A.D. 6, his territory was placed under the control of Roman officials called procurators. The procurator who was in office during Jesus' public ministry was Pontius Pilate. Herod Antipas, with the title of "tetrarch," continued to rule until A.D. 39; Philip until about A.D. 33. The public ministry of Jesus extended from A.D. 26 or 27 to A.D. 29 or 30. During most of that time he was in the territory of Herod Antipas and of Pontius Pilate, though occasionally he entered the territory of Philip.

Matthew 3: 1-12, and Parallels

The beginning of Jesus' public ministry was prepared for by the work of John the Baptist. Matt. 3 : 1–12, and parallels. John was the last and greatest prophet of the old dispensation, who came just before the dawn of the new age. For centuries prophecy had been silent. But at last a prophet came in the spirit and power of Elijah to prepare the heart of the people for the promised Messiah.

Even in dress and in manner of life, John was like a prophet of the olden time. His food was locusts and wild honey; he was clothed with a rough camel's-hair garment; and his preaching was carried on in the deserts. The substance of his message is summed up in the words, "Repent ye; for the kingdom of heaven is at hand." Matt. 3 : 2.

The phrase, "kingdom of heaven," or "kingdom of God," was evidently familiar to the hearers of John, and the meaning of the phrase, up to a certain point, is perfectly clear. As the kingdom of Cæsar is the place where Cæsar bears rule, so the Kingdom of God is the place, or the condition, where God bears rule. In one sense, the whole universe is the Kingdom of God, for nothing happens apart from God's will. But evidently John was using the phrase in some narrower sense; he meant by the Kingdom of God the condition where God's will is wrought out to completion, where the sinful disobedience which prevails in the world is banished and God is truly King.

The Jews expected an age which should be under the perfect control

*of God. But they were surprised by what John the Baptist said about
the requirements for entrance into that age. They had supposed that
all Jews would have the blessing of the Kingdom, but John told them
that only the righteous would be allowed to enter in. It was a startling
message, since the hearers of John knew only too well that they did
not possess the righteousness which was required. Repentance, therefore, or cleansing from sin, was necessary. And the sign of cleansing
was baptism.

Matthew 3: 13 to 4: 11, and Parallels

Among those who came to be baptized was Jesus of Nazareth.
Matt. 3 : 13–15, and parallels. Jesus did not need to be baptized for
his own sake, for he had no sin to be washed away. But his baptism
was part of what he was doing for his people. Just as on the cross he
received the punishment of sin, though there was no sin of his own,
so in his baptism he represented the sinful people whom he came to save.

When Jesus had been baptized, there was a wonderful event which
was perceived not only by him but also by John the Baptist. Matt.
3 : 16, 17, and parallels. The Holy Spirit descended upon him in the
form of a dove, and there was a voice from heaven which said,
"This is my beloved Son, in whom I am well pleased." This event
marks the beginning of Jesus' public ministry as Messiah. He had
been the Messiah already, and he had already possessed the Holy
Spirit; but now the power of the Spirit impelled him to come forward
definitely as the promised One.

At the very beginning, however, there was temptation to be overcome. Matt. 4 : 1–11, and parallels. Jesus was led up from the deep
Jordan Valley, where the baptism had taken place, into the wilderness
on the heights. And there he was tempted. The temptation was based
upon the holy experience which he had just received. The voice from
heaven had designated Jesus as Son of God. "If that be true," said
the Tempter, "if thou art really Son of God, use thy power to obtain
creature comfort, test out thy power by casting thyself down from a
pinnacle of the Temple, obtain the immediate enjoyment of thy power
by doing obeisance to me." The Devil quoted Scripture for his evil
purpose. But Jesus did not need to repudiate the Scripture in order
to refute him. The Holy Scriptures themselves contained a sufficient
answer to every suggestion of the Evil One. The great victory was
won. The Kingdom of the Messiah was not to be a worldly realm, and

it was not to be won by worldly means. The path to the Messiah's, throne led by the way of the cross. And that path our Saviour was willing to tread for our sakes.

QUESTIONS ON LESSON III

1. What is known about the boyhood and youth of Jesus?
2. Describe the physical features and the political divisions of Palestine at the time of our Lord. Where was Jesus born, where did he spend his youth, and where was he baptized?
3. What was the meaning of John's baptism? Why was Jesus baptized?
4. What was the meaning of each of the three temptations, and how did Jesus overcome them?

LESSON IV

The Early Judean Ministry

John 1:19-34

After the temptation Jesus descended again into the Jordan Valley, where the baptism had taken place. There he received the testimony of John the Baptist. John 1 : 19–34. John had come not to perform a work of his own, but to be a witness to the greater One who was to follow. He put aside, therefore, all thoughts of personal ambition, declared plainly that he was not the Christ, and rejoiced when his disciples left him in order to follow the One whom he had come to announce. John had had revealed to him, moreover, not merely the fact that Jesus was the Saviour, but also something of the way in which the salvation was to be wrought. Jesus was to die, like a sacrificial lamb, for the sins of others. "Behold, the Lamb of God," said John to his disciples, "that taketh away the sin of the world!"

John 1:35-51

Two pairs of brothers, in those early days, left John to follow the Saviour. John 1 : 35–42. One pair consisted of Andrew and Peter; the other, no doubt, consisted of the two sons of Zebedee, James and John, although John, who wrote the Gospel in which this narrative is contained, has never mentioned his own name in his book. Two other men, besides these four, came to Jesus on the following day—Philip and Nathanael. Vs. 43–51.

John 2: 1-11

After the meeting with these six disciples, our Lord ascended again from the valley of the Jordan to the higher country of Galilee. And there, in the village of Cana, he wrought the first of his miracles. John 2 : 1–11. He was a guest at a wedding feast, and when the wine ran out he supplied the lack by turning water into wine. Thereby he not only manifested his power, but also indicated the manner of his ministry. He was not to be an austere person like John the Baptist, living far from the habitations of men. On the contrary, his ministry was, for those whom he came to win, a ministry of joy. He entered not merely into the sorrows, but also into the joys of men; the One who was to die for the sins of the world was also willing to grace a marriage feast!

John 2:12-22

After a brief sojourn at Capernaum, on the shores of the Sea of Galilee, where he was afterwards to carry on a large part of his ministry, Jesus went southward to Jerusalem at passover time. At Jerusalem his first recorded act was an act of stern rebuke. John 2 : 13–22. The Temple area was filled with the tables of those who sold the sheep and oxen and doves which were intended for sacrifice; the sacred precincts of God's house had been made a place of business. There was no hesitation on the part of Jesus; he made a scourge of cords and drove the traffickers out. It is a mistake to suppose that the wonderful gentleness of our Saviour or his gracious participation in innocent joys was any indication of weakness. Though always merciful to the penitent, Jesus could be indignant against blatant sinners; and the righteous anger of the Saviour was a terrible thing.

John 2:23-25

At Jerusalem Jesus won adherents because of the miracles which he wrought. But he was able to distinguish true devotion from that which was false. He "knew all men, . . . and needed not that any one should bear witness concerning man; for he himself knew what was in man." John 2 : 24, 25.

John 3:1-15

One example of this knowledge was afforded by the case of Nicodemus, John 3 : 1–15; Jesus knew what Nicodemus lacked. Nico-

demus, a ruler of the Jews, came to Jesus by night, to discuss the substance of what Jesus had been saying. But our Lord would not waste
time with things that lay on the surface. He went straight to the heart
of the matter, and said to Nicodemus, "Ye must be born anew." V. 7.
None of the learning, none of the worldly influence of Nicodemus
would avail; true life could come only by a new birth, which all, rich
and poor, learned and ignorant, must receive, and receive, not by their
own efforts, but by the mysterious power of the Spirit of God. Jesus
spoke, too, on that memorable night, of the sacrificial death which he
himself was to die for the sins of men. "As Moses lifted up the serpent
in the wilderness," he said, "even so must the Son of man be lifted up;
that whosoever believeth may in him have eternal life."

John 3:22-30

Then Jesus left Jerusalem, the capital, and carried on, through his
disciples, a ministry of baptism in the country districts of Judea.
John 3 : 22–30. He was thus engaging in a work which before had
belonged peculiarly to John the Baptist. Some of John's disciples were
perhaps inclined to be envious. But there was no envy in the heart
of John himself. He had come not for his own sake but to be a witness to Jesus as Messiah. And now he rejoiced in the growing promi-
nence of Jesus. "The friend of the bridegroom," he said about himself, "rejoices at the voice of the bridegroom. He must increase, but
I must decrease." Vs. 29, 30, in substance.

John 4:1-42

When this early Judean ministry was over, Jesus went back to
Galilee. On the way he passed through Samaria. John 4 : 1–42.
The inhabitants of Samaria were not of pure Jewish race, and although
they accepted the five books of Moses and looked for the coming of
a Messiah, they did not accept all of the Old Testament. They were
despised by the Jews. But even for the Samaritans, and for the most
degraded among them, the Saviour had a message of hope. Wearied
by his journey, our Lord was sitting by Jacob's well near the city of
Sychar. When his disciples had gone into the city to buy food, a
woman came to draw water at the well. For that woman it was a
memorable hour. Jesus was willing to labor, and that in the midst
of his weariness, for one sinful soul, as well as for all the multitudes
that had crowded around him in Judea. The woman was of sinful

life, and she could not hide her sin from Jesus But Jesus searched out her sin, not in order to condemn her, but in order to bring to her the message of salvation. Attracted, then, by what the woman had said, a number of the Samaritans came to Jesus and recognized him as the Messiah and as the Saviour of the world.

QUESTIONS ON LESSON IV

1. Give an account of the testimony of John the Baptist to Jesus. How did John know that Jesus was the Messiah?
2. What happened at Cana? Who, besides Jesus, was a guest at the feast?
3. Give an outline of all the journeys of Jesus up to his passage through Samaria.
4. Give an account, fuller than the outline given, of the early Judean ministry. What did Jesus say when he was asked to give a sign?
5. What is the meaning of the "new birth"? Is it still necessary to-day if a man is to be saved? How does it come?

LESSON V.
The Beginning of the Galilæan Ministry

After passing through Samaria, Jesus arrived in Galilee, and it was in Galilee that a large part of his ministry was carried on. The Galilæan ministry is narrated for the most part by the first three Gospels, which are called Synoptic Gospels, whereas the Gospel According to John deals more particularly with the work in Judea.

Luke 4: 16-30

After the healing of a nobleman's son, when Jesus was at Cana of Galilee, our Lord began his preaching in the Galilæan synagogues. Early in this period he went to Nazareth, the place where he had been brought up. Luke 4 : 16-30. But the people of Nazareth could not believe that the carpenter's Son whom they had known was really chosen by God to fulfill the glorious prophecies of Isaiah. When rebuked by Jesus they even desired to kill him. Thus did they illustrate, to their own eternal loss, the words of Jesus that "No prophet is acceptable in his own country."

Leaving Nazareth, our Lord went down and dwelt at Capernaum, making that city apparently the center of his work. But before the details of the Galilæan ministry are studied, it will be well to cast a hurried glance at the geographical features of the country where Jesus' ministry was carried on.

The political divisions of Palestine have already been mentioned—Galilee in the north, under the tetrarch, Herod Antipas; Samaria and Judea to the south, under the Roman procurator, Pontius Pilate. But the physical features of the country do not correspond at all to the political divisions. Physically the country is divided into four narrow strips, each about one hundred and fifty miles long, running from north to south. The westernmost strip is the coastal plain, along the Mediterranean Sea, into which Jesus hardly went; then comes the low hill country, the "shephela"; then the highlands, upon which Jerusalem is situated, reaching an altitude of some 2500 feet above sea level. These central highlands of Palestine are broken by the plain of Esdraelon, in southern Galilee. A little to the north of this plain, in a hill country, lies the town of Nazareth. East of the central highlands is the deep valley of the Jordan River. The Jordan rises in the extreme north of Palestine, one of its sources being on the slopes of the lofty Mount Hermon; then flows southward to the lake called "the waters of Merom"; then, issuing from that lake, it flows, after a short course, into the Lake of Gennesaret, or Sea of Galilee, which is about twelve miles long; then, issuing from the Lake of Gennesaret, it flows southward, through a very deep valley to the Dead Sea, which has no outlet and is extremely salt. During most of its course the Jordan Valley lies far below the level of the sea, being on account of this peculiarity absolutely unique among the river valleys of the world. The Dead Sea is 1292 feet, and the Lake of Gennesaret 682 feet, below sea level. It was on the shores of the Lake of Gennesaret that a large part of our Lord's ministry was carried on. Centuries of misrule have now ruined the country, but in those days Galilee supported a large population. The shores of the lake, particularly, were lined with villages and towns. The work of our Lord was thus carried on amid "life's throng and press," though from time to time he sought out the desert places for rest and prayer.

Matthew 4:18-22, and Parallels

At the beginning of the ministry on the shores of the Lake of Galilee, Jesus called the two pairs of brothers—Simon Peter and Andrew, and

James and John. Matt. 4 : 18–22, and parallels. They had known Jesus before, and had devoted themselves to his service. But now they were commanded to show their devotion by leaving their ordinary occupation and becoming Jesus' permanent followers.

Mark 1:21-39, and Parallels

The Gospels give a vivid picture of a Sabbath which Jesus spent at Capernaum near the beginning of his Galilæan ministry. Mark 1 : 21–34, and parallels. As usual, he went into the synagogue. Our Lord knew how to find God's handiwork in the flowers of the field; but he was not like those who think that the worship of God through nature is any substitute for the public worship of the Church. In the synagogue the people were astonished at Jesus' teaching: "He taught them as having authority, and not as the scribes." But they were also astonished at his power; he commanded even the unclean spirits and they obeyed him. He was not merely a teacher, but also a healer; he brought not merely guidance, but also active help.

After the synagogue service, Jesus went into the house of Simon and Andrew with James and John. In the house he healed Simon's wife's mother who was sick of a fever. Others had heard of the wonderful power of Jesus, and desired to be healed. But in order not to break the Sabbath, they waited until sunset, when the Jewish Sabbath was over. At sunset they brought to Jesus those who were sick and those who were possessed with demons, and Jesus put forth his divine power to heal.

It had been a crowded, busy day. Our Lord must have been weary as night at last came. But even in such busy days, he took time to seek the source of all strength. A great while before the dawn he went out into a desert place and there prayed. Mark 1 : 35–39, and parallels.

Matthew 9:1-8, and Parallels

After a tour in the Galilæan synagogues, with both preaching and healing, our Lord returned to Capernaum. There, as is told in one of the vivid narratives of the Gospels, Jesus healed a paralytic. Matt. 9 : 1–8, and parallels. The sick man could not be brought in by the door of the house because of the crowds. But he and his friends were not to be denied. The four friends who bore his couch lowered him through the roof into the place where Jesus was. They had found the Healer at last. But bodily healing was not the first gift which Jesus bestowed. "Son," said Jesus, "thy sins are forgiven." It was a strange physician indeed who could forgive sins. The scribes said that the word of Jesus was blasphemy. And so it was, unless Jesus himself were God. As a proof of his divine power, the Lord said also to the paralytic, "Arise, and take up thy bed, and walk." And so the man went away from the presence of the great Healer, whole in body and in mind.

QUESTIONS ON LESSON V

1. Describe the political and the physical divisions of Palestine. In what parts of the country was our Lord's ministry carried on? Where was Nazareth? Capernaum? Point out these places on a map.
2. Describe the call of the four disciples. When and where had they followed Jesus before? What was their occupation?
3. Give an account of the Sabbath in Capernaum that is described in the Gospels. What great divisions of Jesus' work were illustrated on that day?
4. Describe the healing of the paralytic. What can be learned from this incident about the nature of Jesus' person? Why were the scribes offended?

LESSON VI

The Period of Popularity

During the first part of the Galilæan ministry, our Lord had the favor of the people. Great crowds followed him so that he could scarcely enter into a house. On one occasion he embarked in a little boat and put forth a short distance into the lake, so as to be able to speak to the throng on the shore.

This popularity, it is true, was not universal. The common people heard Jesus gladly, but the official teachers were hostile. These teachers, who are called scribes, belonged for the most part to the sect of the Pharisees. At the time of Christ there were two chief parties among the Jews—the Pharisees and the Sadducees. The Sadducees were a worldly aristocracy, in possession of the high-priestly offices at Jerusalem, favored by the Romans, and satisfied with the existing political order. The Pharisees, on the other hand, were a strict Jewish party, insisted on a strict interpretation of the Mosaic Law, and added to the Law a great mass of oral "tradition," which ostensibly consisted of interpretation of the Law, but really meant an enormous and oppressive addition to it. The Pharisees were opposed to Jesus for at least two reasons. In the first place, they were envious of his success in teaching, which endangered their own position. In the second place, they were opposed to the contents of his teaching; he rejected their interpretation of the Law, and rebuked them for paying such attention to the detailed rules which were set forth in their tradition as to forget the weightier matters of justice and mercy.

The conflict of Jesus with the Pharisees was precipitated particularly by the attitude of Jesus toward the Sabbath. The Sabbath controversy was carried on partly in Galilee and partly, John, ch. 5, during a visit of Jesus to Jerusalem. The Pharisees had developed for the preservation of the Sabbath an elaborate set of rules which went far beyond what was set forth in the Old Testament. They were offended, therefore, when Jesus refused to rebuke his disciples for plucking the ears of wheat on the Sabbath Day, and when he himself insisted on using the Sabbath to perform works of mercy like the healing of the man that had a withered hand.

But for the present the opposition of the Pharisees was held in check by the favor which our Lord had among the people.

This favor was due partly to the teaching of Jesus and partly to his miracles. He interpreted the Scriptures in a fresh, original way; "He taught as one having authority and not as their scribes." And he had power to heal every manner of disease and to cast out demons. It was no wonder that the crowds followed so wonderful a teacher.

Matthew 4:17

The Galilæan teaching of Jesus began with the proclamation of the Kingdom of God. The message sounded at first somewhat like the message of John the Baptist. Quite like John, Jesus came forward with the summons, "Repent ye; for the kingdom of heaven is at hand." But the new teacher differed from John in the more complete account which he gave of the nature of the Kingdom, and especially in the central place in the Kingdom which he assigned to himself.

Matthew, Chapters 5 to 7

The nature of the Kingdom of God is set forth in the great discourse of our Lord which is commonly called the Sermon on the Mount.

Matt., chs. 5 to 7. Having gone up from the shores of the Sea of
Galilee to the heights which surround the lake, our Lord taught his
disciples what was to be the life of those who should have a part
in the Kingdom of God. In one sense, the Kingdom lay altogether in
the future; it would be ushered in with full power only at the end
of the world. But in another sense, it was present already wherever
there were those who were truly submitting their lives to Jesus.

The Sermon on the Mount contains certain features which are
fundamental in all of Jesus' teaching.

In the first place, God is presented, in the Sermon on the Mount,
as "Father." The fatherhood of God, in the teaching of Jesus, is sometimes misunderstood. Jesus did not mean that God is Father of all
men. God stands indeed to all men in a relation which is analogous
to that of a father to his children; he cares for all, he makes his sun to
rise upon all. Matt. 5 : 45. But in the teaching of Jesus and in the
whole New Testament the lofty term, "Father," is reserved for a
still more intimate relationship. So in the Sermon on the Mount
the great world without is sharply distinguished from the company
of Jesus' disciples; it is only the latter who can say, "Our Father which
art in heaven."

There was nothing narrow in such teaching; for although in Jesus'
teaching the intimate relation of sonship toward God was offered
only to those who should be of the household of faith, yet the door
of the household of faith was open wide to all who would be willing
to come in. Indeed Jesus himself died on the cross with the purpose
of opening that door. Our Saviour did far more than teach men that
they were already children of God; he came to make them children
of God by his saving work.

In the second place, the Sermon on the Mount tells what kind of
life is led by those who should have entered into the Kingdom and
been made the children of God. That life is far more than obedience
to a set of external rules; the purity which Jesus demanded is a purity
of the heart. The life in the Kingdom is also far removed from all
pretense; the children of God engage in prayer and good works not
to be seen by men but to be seen by God. Finally, the life in the
Kingdom is a life of perfect trust; all anxious thought for the morrow is
banished, since God will care for his children.

One difficulty arises in the reading of the Sermon on the Mount.
How can such an ideal be attained? It might be possible to obey a

set of rules, like the rules of the Pharisees, but how is it possible for sinful men to attain purity of heart? The righteousness of the Kingdom of heaven exceeds by far the "righteousness of the scribes and Pharisees." How can such righteousness be attained?

The answer to this question was partly understood even by the first hearers of the Sermon on the Mount. The disciples of Jesus knew even then that Jesus alone could give them entrance into the Kingdom; they trusted in him already not merely as teacher but also as Saviour. But the answer to the question is far plainer to us; for we know the cross. The atoning death of Christ it was that gave men the kind of righteousness required for entrance into the Kingdom of God, for it gave them the righteousness of Christ himself. The significance of the cross was spoken of by our Lord even during his earthly ministry, but the full explanation of it was left to the apostles. The saving work of Jesus could be fully explained only after it had been done.

QUESTIONS ON LESSON VI

1. What is the meaning of "the kingdom of God," in Jesus' teaching?
2. Who were the Sadducees? Who were the Pharisees, and why were they opposed to Jesus?
3. Give an outline of the Sermon on the Mount.

LESSON VII
The Turning Point

The teaching of Jesus was carried on in various ways. Sometimes there were extended discourses like the Sermon on the Mount. On the other hand, much of the most precious teaching of our Lord is contained in brief sayings which were uttered in answer to some objection or in view of some special situation. One other form of teaching requires special attention—namely, the parables.

Mark 4:1-34, and Parallels

A parable is a narrative taken from ordinary life, but intended to teach some spiritual lesson. It differs from an allegory in that the application is not to be carried out in such detail. Ordinarily a parable teaches simply one lesson; there is only one point of similarity between the literal meaning of the parable and the deeper spiritual truth. Thus when our Lord compared God's answer to prayer with the answer which an unjust judge gives to an importunate widow, the details in the two cases are not intended to be similar; God is very different from the unjust judge. But there is one point of similarity —importunity does have its effect in both cases.

The distinction between a parable and an allegory is not an absolute distinction, and sometimes the two shade into each other. Thus the parable of the Wicked Husbandmen, which Jesus uttered nearly at the close of his earthly ministry, partakes largely of the nature of allegory. The details to a considerable extent are significant—the wicked husbandmen represent the Jews and their leaders, the servants who were first sent represent the prophets, the son who was sent last represents Jesus himself. But many of Jesus' parables are parables pure and simple; they are not intended to be pressed in detail, but teach, each of them, some one lesson.

The purpose of Jesus in using parables was twofold. In the first place the parables were not clear to those who did not wish to learn. In accordance with a principle of the divine justice, willful closing of the eyes to the truth brought an increase of darkness. But in the second place, to those who were willing to receive the truth, the parables were made gloriously plain; the figurative form of the teaching only served to drive the meaning home.

The ministry of Jesus did not consist merely of teaching. Along with the teaching there went wonderful manifestations of divine power. These manifestations of divine power were of various kinds. Many of them were miracles of healing; Jesus had power to make the lame to walk, the dumb to speak, the deaf to hear. He also had power to cast out demons. At the presence of the Son of God, Satan and his ministers had put forth all their baneful power. But the demons were obliged to flee at Jesus' word.

Matthew 8: 23-27, and Parallels

Not all of the miracles, however, were miracles of healing. Some of the most notable of them were of a different kind. But all of them were manifestations of Jesus' divine power. When, on the lake, in the midst of the frightened disciples, our Lord said to the winds and the waves, "Peace, be still," the Ruler of all nature was revealed. The particular form of Jesus' miracles depended upon his own inscrutable will; but all of the miracles revealed him as the Master of the world. He who had made the world in the beginning could still put forth the same creative power. A miracle, as distinguished from the ordinary course of nature, is a manifestation of the creative, as distinguished from the providential, power of God.

Matthew 14: 13-21, and Parallels

Among the miracles of Jesus the feeding of the five thousand seems to have been particularly important. Its importance is indicated by the fact that it is narrated in all four of the Gospels. Matt. 14 : 13-21, and parallels. Even the Gospel of John, which is concerned for the most part with what happened in Judea, here runs parallel with the Synoptic Gospels and narrates an event which happened in Galilee.

This event marks the climax of the popularity of our Lord and at the same time the beginning of his rejection. Even before this time he had been rejected by some; his popularity had been by no means universal. He had been opposed by the scribes and Pharisees; he had not been understood even by the members of his own household; and he had been rejected twice at the town where he had been brought up. But for the most part he had enjoyed the favor of the people.

At the time of the feeding of the five thousand, this popular favor had reached its height. Jesus had withdrawn from the crowds into a lonely place across the lake from Capernaum. But such was his popularity that he could not escape. The people followed him even when he tried to be alone; they had had no thought of food or of lodging for the night, so eager had they been to listen to his teaching. When evening came, therefore, they were in want. But our Lord had pity on them because they were like sheep without a shepherd. By a gracious manifestation of his divine power he made the five loaves and two fishes suffice for all the multitude.

Matthew 14: 22-34, and Parallels

After the feeding of the five thousand Jesus found at last the solitude which he had sought; he went up into the mountain to pray. The multitudes were making their way around the lake by the shore; the disciples had taken the only boat and were rowing hard against the wind. But about three o'clock at night our Lord came to the disciples walking upon the water. It is no wonder that they bowed before him and said, "Of a truth thou art the Son of God."

John 6: 22-71

Meanwhile the multitude had gone on foot around the lake to Capernaum. When they found Jesus there before them they were astonished. But their astonishment, unfortunately, was not of the kind that leads to true and abiding faith. They had valued the earthly bread which Jesus had given them, but were not willing to receive the spiritual bread. Jesus himself, he told them, was the Bread of life who had come down from heaven; only those could truly live who would feed upon him by accepting his saving work. John 6 : 22–71.

It seemed to the Jews to be a hard saying. How could the Jesus whose family they knew be the bread which had come down from heaven? Many even of those who had formerly followed Jesus were offended at this "hard saying." The popularity of Jesus at this time began to wane.

But there were some disciples who remained. Jesus had chosen twelve men, whom he called apostles. He had had them as his companions, and already he had sent them out on a mission to teach and to heal. Turning now to them, he asked, "Would ye also go away?" Then Peter, speaking for the others, showed the difference between true disciples and those who are offended at every hard saying. "Lord," he said, "to whom shall we go? thou hast the words of eternal life."

QUESTIONS ON LESSON VII

1. What is a parable? How does it differ from an allegory?
2. Why did Jesus use parables? Mention some of the parables recorded in the Gospels.
3. What is a miracle? Why did Jesus work miracles?
4. What is the particular importance of the feeding of the five thousand?
5. Why were the people offended by the discourse on the Bread of life?

LESSON VIII

Jesus as Messiah

The waning of Jesus' popularity was by no means sudden. Even after the discourse on the Bread of life, we frequently find the multitudes around him. But in general, from that time on our Lord seems to have withdrawn from the crowds more frequently than before, in order to devote himself to the instruction of his intimate disciples.

Matthew 15:21-39, and Parallels

At this time our Lord withdrew into Phœnicia, northwest of Palestine. In Phœnicia he healed the daughter of a Syrophœnician woman. It was a foretaste of the rich streams of mercy which after Pentecost were to flow out into the whole world.

After a brief stay in Phœnicia, Jesus returned to Galilee, where he engaged again in controversy with the Pharisees and again, by his divine power, fed a great multitude. This second time four thousand men were fed. There were also miracles of healing, and in general the essential characteristics of the Galilæan ministry were continued.

Matthew 16:13-20, and Parallels

But before long Jesus departed again from Galilee, and finally went with his disciples to the regions of Cæsarea Philippi, northeast of Galilee. Near Cæsarea Philippi occurred the great confession of Peter, which is one of the most important incidents of the Gospel record. Matt. 16 : 13–20, and parallels.

"Who," Jesus asked of his disciples, "do men say that I am? And they told him, saying, Elijah; but others, One of the prophets. And he asked them, But who say ye that I am? Peter answereth and saith unto him, Thou art the Christ." Mark 8 : 27–29.

In this confession Peter recognized that Jesus was the "Messiah," the "Anointed One," or according to the Greek translation of the same word, "the Christ." It was by no means the first recognition of the fact. The Messiahship of Jesus had been revealed to Joseph and Mary and Zacharias and Elisabeth even before Jesus was born; it had been revealed to the shepherds and the Wise Men who greeted the infant Saviour; it had been revealed to John the Baptist; it had been revealed to the little group of disciples who left John at the Jordan in order to follow Jesus; it had been proclaimed by Jesus himself in his conversations with Nicodemus and with the Samaritan woman; it had been recognized even by the unclean spirits.

But although Jesus had been proclaimed as Messiah before, the confession of Peter was by no means a matter of course. Although the disciples had already accepted Jesus as the Messiah it required considerable faith and devotion to continue to accept him, for Jesus was not the kind of Messiah whom the Jews had been expecting. They had been expecting a Messiah who, as anointed king of Israel, would deliver God's people from the Roman oppressors, and make Jerusalem the center of the whole world.   .

Such expectations seemed to be set at nought by the Prophet of Nazareth. No kingly pomp surrounded him; he mingled freely with the common people; he lived in the utmost humility, having not even a place to lay his head. Political Messiahship he definitely refused. When, after the feeding of the five thousand, the people were about to come and make him a king—that is, the Messianic king—he left them and withdrew into the mountain. John 6 : 15. It is no wonder that they were disappointed. All their enthusiasm seemed to be ruthlessly quenched. Jesus would have absolutely nothing to do with the kind of Messiahship which they offered.

By this attitude of Jesus not only the multitudes were discouraged. Even the members of Jesus' household failed to understand, and the very forerunner of Jesus, John the Baptist himself, was assailed, momentarily at least, by doubts. Conceivably the twelve apostles also might have been discouraged. But their faith remained firm. Despite all disappointments, despite the refusal of our Lord to accept what were supposed to be prerogatives of Messiahship, Peter was able still to say, at Cæsarea Philippi, "Thou art the Christ."

But in what sense was Jesus the Christ? He was not an earthly king who would lead the armies of Israel out to battle against the Romans. He was not that sort of Messiah. What then was he? What was Jesus' own conception of Messiahship?

In order to answer that question fully, it would be necessary to return to the study of the Old Testament. Jesus accepted to the full the Old Testament promises about the Messiah; what he rejected was merely a false interpretation of them.

Even those promises of the Old Testament which make the Messiah a king of David's line were fulfilled in Jesus. He was actually of David's line, and he was born in David's city. He was also the King of Israel.

Only his kingship was exercised in ways different from those which the people generally were expecting. And there were other features of the Old Testament promises which Jesus also fulfilled. Jesus was not only Son of David; he was also Son of Man. The title "Son of Man," which was Jesus' own Messianic designation of himself, does not denote merely the humanity of Jesus in distinction from his deity. On the contrary, it is plainly taken from the stupendous scene in Dan. 7 : 13, where "one like unto a son of man" is represented as coming with the clouds of heaven, and as being in the presence of God. It indicates, therefore, not the human weakness of Jesus, but his exalted position as supreme Ruler and Judge.

It is not surprising that for a time at least during his earthly ministry Jesus used this title of the Messiah rather than the other titles, for the title Son of Man was without the political associations which Jesus desired to avoid. It had been employed, not so much by the masses of the people, as by the circles which read the books which are called the "Apocalypses." In these books, on the basis of Daniel and other Old Testament prophecies, the Messiah was represented not as a political king, but as a heavenly, supernatural person. The title, therefore, was admirably fitted to designate the lofty character of the Messiah's person, without the dangerous political associations which had gathered around certain other titles.

Indeed for a time, in the early Galilæan ministry, our Lord seems to have kept his Messiahship somewhat in the background. Public proclamation of his Messiahship would have aroused false, worldly hopes of political upheaval. Before proclaiming himself again as Messiah, our Lord needed to make clear by his teaching and by his example what kind of Messiah he was; before finally setting up his Kingdom he needed to show that that Kingdom was nqt of this world. But he was Messiah and King from the beginning, and even at the beginning his Messiahship had been made known.

QUESTIONS ON LESSON VIII

1. Mention some of the titles which are used to designate Jesus as Messiah, and explain their meaning. Was the title "Son of Man" ever used with reference to Jesus by anyone except Jesus himself?
2. What was the significance of Peter's confession?
3. Why did Jesus become less popular than he was at first?

LESSON IX

The Prediction of the Cross

Peter's confession at Cæsarea Philippi was a triumph of faith, for which Jesus pronounced Peter blessed. Through a revelation from God, Peter had been made able to endure the disappointment involved in Jesus' refusal of kingly honors. But another trial of faith was soon to come.

Matthew 16:21-28, and Parallels

After Peter's acknowledgment of Jesus as Messiah, our Lord began
to teach the disciples more of what his Messiahship meant. Matt.
16 : 21–28, and parallels. It meant, he said, not worldly honors,
and not merely a continuation of the humble life in Galilee, but actual
sufferings and death. This teaching was more than Peter could endure.
"Be it far from thee, Lord," he said, "this shall never be unto thee."
In such rebellion against God's will Jesus recognized a repetition
of the temptation which had come to him at the first, immediately
after the voice from heaven had proclaimed him to be the Messiah—
the temptation to use his Messianic power for his own worldly glory.
And now as well as then the temptation was resolutely overcome.
"Get thee behind me, Satan," said Jesus: "thou art a stumbling-
block unto me: for thou mindest not the things of God, but the things
of men."

Jesus was thus ready to tread the path of suffering which he had
come into the world, for our sakes, to tread. And he called upon his
true disciples to tread that path after him. Yet all the suffering was
to be followed by a greater glory than Peter had ever conceived; and
almost immediately there was a wonderful foretaste of that glory.

Matthew 17:1-13, and Parallels

Six days after the scene at Cæsarea Philippi, our Lord took Peter
and James and John, his three most intimate disciples, with him up
upon a high mountain—no doubt somewhere on the slopes of the lofty
Mount Hermon. There he was transfigured before them, Matt. 17 :
1–13, and parallels; "his face did shine as the sun, and his garments
became white as the light." With him appeared Moses and Elijah,
talking with him. And they were talking about what seems to be a
strange subject at such a moment. They were talking not of the
glories of Jesus' Kingdom, but of the "departure" which he was about
to accomplish at Jerusalem. Luke 9 : 31. The "departure" included
not only the resurrection and the ascension, but also the crucifixion.
Even the shining light of the transfiguration was intended to point
to the cross.

Matthew 17:14-20, and Parallels

After the glorious experience on the mountain, our Lord came at
once into contact with the repulsiveness of human misery. Matt.

17 : 14–20, and parallels. But he did not shrink from the sudden transition. As he came down from the mountain, he found at the bottom a boy possessed of a demon, who "fell on the ground, and wallowed foaming." It was a depressing sight, very unlike the brightness of the transfiguration. Even more discouraging, moreover, than the condition of the boy himself was the powerlessness of the disciples. They had tried to cast the demon out but had failed miserably, not because the power might not have been theirs, but because of their unbelief. The father of the boy, too, was lacking in faith. "I believe," he said; "help thou mine unbelief." Jesus did help his unbelief, and the unbelief of the disciples. He rebuked the unclean spirit, and healed the boy.

At this period Jesus repeated on several occasions the prophecy of his death. The tragedy on Calvary did not overtake him unawares. He went deliberately to his death for our sakes.

Matthew 18: 1-6, and Parallels

Even on such solemn days, when the shadow of the cross lay over the path, the disciples were unable to overcome the pettiness of their character. On the very journey when Jesus had told them about his approaching death, they had quarreled about the question as to which of them should be greatest in the Kingdom of heaven. Thereby they had shown how far they were from understanding the true nature of the Kingdom. If the Kingdom was finally to be advanced under the leadership of such men, some mighty change would have to take place in them. That change did take place afterwards, as we shall see, at Pentecost. But at present the pettiness and carnal-mindedness of the disciples added to the sorrows of our Lord. Despite the intimacy into which he entered with his earthly friends, he towered in lonely grandeur above them all.

After the transfiguration and related events near Cæsarea Philippi, our Lord returned to Galilee. But apparently he did not resume permanently his Galilæan ministry. Soon we find him passing through Samaria, and laboring in Judea and in that country east of the Jordan River which is called Perea. This part of Jesus' ministry is recorded particularly in the Gospels According to Luke and According to John, although Matthew and Mark contain important information about the latter part of the period. The general character of the period is fixed by the expectation of the cross. Jesus had set his face toward

Jerusalem to accomplish the atoning work which he had come into the world to perform.

Luke 10:1-24; John, Chapter 5

At the beginning of the period Jesus sent out seventy disciples, to prepare for his own coming into the several cities and villages which he was intending to visit. The Seventy were in possession of something of Jesus' power; they were able to report with joy that the demons were subjected to them.

During the same period we find Jesus in Jerusalem at the feast of tabernacles. Even during the period of the Galilæan ministry Jesus had gone up to Jerusalem at least once, at the time of one of the Jewish feasts; and in connection with the healing of a man at the pool of Bethesda he had then set forth the true nature of his person and his relation to God the Father. John, ch. 5. At the later period with which we are now dealing, the same teaching was continued. Chs. 7, 8.

Matthew 11:27, and Parallels

It is particularly the Gospel of John which records the way in which Jesus set forth the nature of his own person, but what is fully set forth in the Gospel of John is really implied all through the Synoptic Gospels, and in Matt. 11 : 27; Luke 10 : 22 it is made just as plain as it is in John. According to his own teaching, Jesus stood in a relation toward God the Father which is absolutely different from that in which other men stand toward God. In the plainest possible way, our Lord laid claim to true deity. "I and my Father," he said, "are one." All the Gospels present the true humanity of Jesus, the Gospel According to John, no less than the Synoptists. But all the Gospels also set forth his deity. He was, according to a true summary of the Gospel teaching, "God and man, in two distinct natures, and one person for ever."

QUESTIONS ON LESSON IX

1. What trial of Peter's faith came just after his great confession?
2. What was the meaning of the transfiguration?
3. What event took place just afterwards?
4. Give an account of Jesus' teaching at the time of the feast of tabernacles. John, chs. 7, 8. How was this teaching received?
5. Give an account of the mission of the Seventy and compare it with the previous mission of the Twelve.

LESSON X
The Last Journeys
John, Chapter 9

During the latter part of Jesus' ministry, with which Lesson IX began to deal, Jesus spoke some of the most beautiful of his parables. A number of them, such as the Good Samaritan and the Prodigal Son, are recorded only by Luke. From the same period the Gospel According to John records some notable teaching of Jesus, in addition to that which was mentioned in the last lesson. Part of this teaching was introduced by the healing of the man born blind. John, ch. 9. This miracle, which had been performed on the Sabbath, had aroused the special opposition of the Pharisees. In answer to them, our Lord pointed out the difference between those leaders of the people who are like robbers breaking into the sheepfold or at best like hirelings who flee at the first approach of danger, and the good shepherd who is willing to lay down his life for the sheep. Such a shepherd was Jesus himself, and his life was soon to be laid down.

John 11:1-53

Finally, after various journeyings of Jesus in Judea and in Perea, there occurred in Bethany, a little village near Jerusalem, one of the most notable of our Lord's miracles. John 11 : 1–44. At Bethany lived a certain Lazarus with his sisters Martha and Mary, whom Jesus knew well. Lazarus fell ill during the absence of Jesus across the Jordan in Perea; and the illness resulted in his death. On the fourth day after Lazarus' death, Jesus came to Bethany. Martha came to meet him; Mary remained mourning in the house, until her sister brought word that Jesus had arrived. Then she, too, went to meet the Lord. When Jesus saw her and her friends weeping for the one who had died, he, too, wept with them. But he had power not only to sympathize, but also to help. Going with the sisters to the tomb, he caused the stone to be removed, then prayed, and then called with a loud voice, "Lazarus, come forth." At the word of Jesus, the dead man came out of the tomb. Jesus was Master over death and the grave.

It was not the first time that our Lord had raised the dead. He had raised the daughter of Jairus in Galilee and the son of the widow of Nain. But the raising of Lazarus is especially important, not only because of the wonderfully vivid way in which the incident is narrated in the Gospel According to John, but also because it served to hasten the crisis in Jerusalem. Both the Sadducees and the Pharisees were now aroused. The movement instituted by Jesus had reached alarming proportions. If allowed to continue it would be full of danger. The Romans, it was feared, would regard it as rebellion and would utterly destroy the nation of the Jews. The diverse parties among the Jewish leaders were becoming more and more united against the strange Prophet from Galilee.

John 11: 54

For a short time still the crisis was delayed. Our Lord retired from Judea to a city called Ephraim, near the wilderness. We also find him, in this period of his life, again beyond the Jordan, in Perea. In this Perean residence is to be placed a portion of the teaching contained in the Synoptic Gospels, such as the teaching concerning divorce, Matt. 19 : 3–12, and parallels, the words to the rich young ruler, vs. 16–30, and parallels, and the parable of the Laborers in the Vineyard. Matt. 20 : 1–16.

Luke 19: 2-10

Before long, however, Jesus went up to Jerusalem for the last time. On the way, when he was passing through Jericho, in the Jordan Valley, he healed two blind men, and converted the tax collector Zacchæus. The conversion of Zacchæus was in accord with Jesus' custom all through his ministry. The taxgatherers were despised by the rest of the Jews at the time of Christ. They had allied themselves with the Roman oppressors, and no doubt most of them were guilty of abominable extortion on their own account. By the Pharisees, particularly, they were regarded as belonging to the very dregs of the people, with whom no true observer of the law could be intimate. But Jesus was bound by no limits in his saving work. He did not condone sin—either the sin of the taxgatherers or the sin of the Pharisees. But he was willing to save from sin all who would believe. The whole, he said, need not a physician, but they that are sick. The Son of Man had come to "seek and to save that which was lost."

John 11:55 to 12:1

Toiling up the long ascent from Jericho, our Lord arrived at last, six days before the passover, at the village of Bethany, which is less than two miles from Jerusalem. During the remaining time before the crucifixion Jesus went every morning into the city and returned in the evening to lodge with his friends at Bethany.

Matthew 26:6-13, and Parallels

Soon after his arrival at Bethany, when Jesus was reclining at table in the house of a certain Simon the leper, he was anointed by Mary the sister of Lazarus. Matt. 26 : 6–13; Mark 14 : 3–9; John 12 : 2–8. This anointing is not to be confused with a somewhat similar event which had taken place some time before, when Jesus had been anointed by a woman who had been a notorious sinner. Luke 7 : 36–50. The disciples murmured at the waste. The precious ointment, they said, might have been sold for a great sum, which could have been distributed to the poor. Judas Iscariot, one of the Twelve, had a special cause for dissatisfaction; in his case the mention of the poor was only a cloak for covetousness. Judas kept the bag, and if the proceeds of the ointment had been put into his keeping, he could have indulged his thieving propensities. But all the murmuring, whether it proceeded from more sordid motives or from a mere misunderstanding of the true spirit of the woman's act, was rebuked by our Lord. The woman, he said, had anointed his body beforehand for the burial. The days just before the crucifixion were no time for true disciples to murmur at an act which was prompted by overflowing love for the Saviour who was so soon to die.

Matthew 21:1-11, and Parallels

On the day after the supper at Bethany, that is, on the day after the Jewish Sabbath, on the ninth day of the Jewish spring month Nisan, our Lord entered into Jerusalem. Matt. 21 : 1–11, and parallels. It was a triumphal entry; Jesus was received publicly by the multitudes as the Messiah, the promised King of Israel. Even the manner of his entry was in accordance with prophecy; he came riding over the Mount of Olives and into the city mounted on an ass, in accordance with Zech. 9 : 9. The promised King of Israel at last had come. The multitudes strewed palm branches in the way, and cried, "Hosanna to the son of David."

QUESTIONS ON LESSON X

1. Where was Perea? Jericho? Bethany? Ephraim? Find on a map the places mentioned in this lesson.

2. Give an account of all the times when Jesus, during his earthly ministry, raised the dead. In what Gospels are these incidents narrated?
3. What is the special importance of the raising of Lazarus?
4. Give an account of some of those parables of Jesus which are contained only in the Gospel According to Luke.

LESSON XI
Teaching in the Temple

Despite the enthusiasm which the multitudes had shown at the time when Jesus entered into Jerusalem, despite the shouts of those who cried, "Blessed is he that cometh in the name of the Lord," Jesus knew that he was going to his death, and that Jerusalem would soon turn against her King. "When he drew nigh," we are told in the Gospel According to Luke, "he saw the city and wept over it, saying, If thou hadst known in this day, even thou, the things which belong unto peace! but now they are hid from thine eyes." Luke 19 : 41, 42.

On the Sunday of the triumphal entry it was already late when Jesus entered into the Temple area. He did nothing, therefore, that day, except look about him; and then he returned to Bethany with the twelve apostles. Mark 11 : 11.

Matthew 21:12-19, and Parallels

On Monday, however, the final conflict began. Entering into the city, our Lord cast out of the Temple those who bought and sold, just as he had done at the beginning of his public ministry. The rebuke which he had administered several years before had had no permanent effect. But Jesus did not hesitate to rebuke again those who made God's house a place of business. The rulers, of course, were incensed. But popular favor for a time put a check upon their hate. On the way into the city, Jesus said to a fig tree, which was bearing leaves only, "No man eat fruit from thee henceforward for ever." The motives of our Lord's act are not fully known to us; but at least he was able afterwards to point out through the case of the fig tree the limitless power of faith. The disciples were exhorted to pray in faith. But their prayers, Jesus said, must be in love; no unforgiving spirit should be left in their souls when they prayed to their heavenly Father for their own forgiveness.

The next day, Tuesday, was a day of teaching. Our Lord spent the day in the Temple, meeting the attacks of his enemies. And he had an answer to every inquiry; the trick questions of his enemies always redounded to their own rebuke.

Matthew 21:23-32, and Parallels

First our Lord was questioned as to the authority by which he had cleansed the Temple the day before. Matt. 21 : 23–32, and parallels. He answered that question by another question: "The baptism of John, whence was it? from heaven or from men?" The chief priests and elders could not say. They were not really sincere seekers for divine authority. But Jesus was not content with having silenced them. He also pointed out, positively, their sin in not receiving the word of God which had come through John.

Matthew 21:33-46, and Parallels

Still more scathing was the rebuke which Jesus uttered through the parable of the Wicked Husbandmen. Matt. 21 : 33–46, and parallels. The wicked husbandmen had been put in charge of a vineyard. But when the time came to render the fruit of the vineyard to the owner, they killed the servants who were sent to them and finally the owner's son. The chief priests and Pharisees needed no elaborate explanation; they would probably in any case have applied the parable to themselves. But as a matter of fact Jesus made the application abundantly plain. "The kingdom of God," he said, "shall be taken away from you, and shall be given to a nation bringing forth the fruits thereof."

Matthew 22:1-14

Just as plainly directed against the wicked leaders of the people, and against the rebellious nation itself, was the parable of the Marriage of the King's Son. Matt. 22 : 1–14. Those who were bidden to the feast refused to come in; but from the highways and hedges the king's house was filled. So the covenant people, the Jews, had rejected the divine invitation; but the despised Gentiles would be received.

Matthew 22:15-40, and Parallels

The rulers would have liked to put Jesus to death at once; but they still feared the people. So they adopted the underhand method of trying to catch him in his speech. First came the Pharisees and the

Herodians, the latter being the partisans of the Herodian dynasty, with their adroit question about giving tribute to Cæsar, Matt. 22 : 15–22, and parallels; then the Sadducees, the worldly aristocracy, who did not believe in the resurrection, with their attempt to make the doctrine of the resurrection ridiculous, vs. 23–33, and parallels; then an individual Pharisee with his question about the greatest commandment in the law. Vs. 24–40, and parallels. Jesus had a wonderful, profound answer for them all. But only the last inquirer seems to have been at all willing to learn. "Thou art not far," Jesus said to him, "from the kingdom of God." Mark 12 : 34.

Matthew 22:41-46, and Parallels

Then, after all the questions which had been put to him, our Lord put one question in turn. "David himself," he said in effect, "calls the Messiah Lord; how is the Messiah, then, David's son?" In this way Jesus was presenting to the people a higher conception of Messiahship than that which they had been accustomed to hold. The Messiah was indeed David's Son, but he was not only David's Son. Matt. 22 : 41–46, and parallels.

Apparently on the same day, our Lord called attention to the poor widow who was casting her mite into the collection box. A gift, he said, is measured in the estimation of God not by its amount, but by the sacrifice which it means to the giver. Mark 12 : 41–44, and parallel.

Matthew, Chapter 23

Finally, on the same memorable Tuesday, our Lord denounced openly the formalism and hypocrisy of the scribes and Pharisees. Matt., ch. 23. It was also perhaps on the same day that certain Greeks desired to see Jesus, John 12 : 20, 21—a foretaste of that entrance of Gentiles into the Church which was to come after the resurrection. We are not told exactly how Jesus received the Greeks, but the importance of the moment was marked by a voice from heaven which came as a divine confirmation of Jesus' message.

Matthew, Chapters 24, 25

When Jesus, on the same day, had gone out of the Temple and had ascended to the Mount of Olives, a hill which lay on the way to Bethany, he taught his disciples about the coming destruction of the Temple and also about the end of the world. Matt., ch. 24, and parallels. The time of the end of the world, he said, is unknown to all except God, and in expectation of it men should always be watchful. This duty of watchfulness he illustrated by the parables of the Ten Virgins, Matt. 25 : 1–13, and of the Talents. Vs. 14–30. Then our Lord drew a great picture of the last awful judgment of God, when the wicked shall be separated from the good. Vs. 31–46.

QUESTIONS ON LESSON XI

1. Where was the Mount of Olives? Describe the route between Bethany and the Temple in Jerusalem.
2. Compare the two occasions when Jesus cleansed the Temple.
3. On what occasions during his ministry did Jesus speak about John the Baptist?
4. Give a full account of the questions which were put to Jesus on the Tuesday of the last week, and of the answers of Jesus.
5. What were the "woes" which Jesus pronounced against the scribes and Pharisees?
6. What did Jesus say after the Gentiles came to seek him?

LESSON XII

The Crucifixion

Matthew 26:1-5, 14-16, and Parallels

On the Wednesday of the week before the crucifixion, the chief priests and elders of the Jews took counsel how they might put Jesus to death. The difficulty was that if they arrested so popular a teacher in the midst of the crowds who had come to Jerusalem for the approaching feast of the passover, there would be a tumult. At first, therefore, the enemies of Jesus thought that they might have to wait until the passover was over. But they were helped out of their difficulty by one of Jesus' own friends. Judas Iscariot, one of the twelve apostles, proved to be a traitor. He received a promise of thirty pieces of silver, and watched for a time when Jesus would be away from the crowds so that he could be delivered quietly into the hands of his enemies Matt. 26 : 1–5, 14–16, and parallels.

Matthew 26:17-19, and Parallels

Meanwhile, on Thursday, Jesus arranged for the celebration of the passover in company with the apostles. The passover feast commemorated the deliverance of Israel from Egypt, especially the passing over of Israel's first-born when the first-born sons of the Egyptians were slain. The feast was opened on the evening of Nisan 14, Nisan being a spring month, and the first month of the Jewish year. According to Jewish reckoning, the evening of Nisan 14 constituted the beginning of Nisan 15. Starting from that time, the feast continued for seven days, no unleavened bread being used within that period. The first and most solemn act of the whole feast was the eating of the paschal lamb on the evening of Nisan 14.

This passover supper was celebrated by Jesus and the apostles on Thursday evening, Nisan 14. And the feast was to be continued into the Christian era. The symbols were changed; bread and wine were to be used instead of the paschal lamb. But the fundamental meaning of the feast remained the same; both the passover and the Lord's Supper had reference to the atoning death of Christ. The paschal lamb prefigured the Lamb of God who was to die for the sins of the world; the bread and wine also symbolized the body of Christ broken for us and the blood of Christ poured out for the remission of our sins. Thus what the passover symbolized by way of prophecy is symbolized in the Lord's Supper by way of commemoration. And on that last evening our Lord changed the symbols in order to suit the new dispensation when, since the Lamb of God had once been offered up, other sacrifices should be no more.

Matthew 26:20-35, and Parallels

Jesus gathered with his apostles for the feast in an upper room. Matt. 26 : 20, and parallels. Then, lamentably enough, there was a strife among the apostles as to who should be the greatest. Luke 22 : 24-30. As a rebuke of all such inordinate ambitions our Lord gave an example of humility by washing the feet of his disciples. John 13 : 1-20. The traitor, Judas Iscariot, then left the apostolic company, John 13 : 21-35, and parallels, and the Lord's Supper was instituted. I Cor. 11 : 23-25; Matt. 26 : 26-29, and parallels. Then the denial of Peter was foretold; before the cock should crow twice Peter would deny his Lord three times.

John, Chapters 14 to 17

Then followed some of the most precious teaching of Jesus—teaching which is preserved only in the Gospel According to John. Chs. 14 to 17. Our Lord spoke of the mission which he had come into the world to fulfill and of the mission which his apostles were to fulfill through the power of the Holy Spirit. The meaning of Jesus' redeeming work could not fully be explained until it had been accomplished. And it was to be explained by the Holy Spirit speaking through the apostles.

Matthew 26:36-46, and Parallels

After they had sung a hymn, our Lord went out with the eleven apostles to the Garden of Gethsemane, outside of Jerusalem, on the slopes of the Mount of Olives. Matt. 26 : 36–46, and parallels. There he sought strength in prayer for the approaching hour when he was to bear the penalty of our sins. The disciples were no help to him in his agony; Peter and James and John slept while he prayed. But God the Father heard his prayer.

Matthew 26:47 to 27:1

Soon the traitor came with the Temple guard, and Jesus was arrested, Matt. 26 : 47–56, and parallels. On the same evening there was an informal hearing of the Prisoner in the house of Annas, the father-in-law of Caiaphas, the high priest. Matt. 26 : 57, 58, 69–75, and parallels. Meanwhile Peter and "another disciple," who was no doubt John the son of Zebedee, the writer of the Fourth Gospel, had entered into the house. There Peter denied his Lord.

The next morning there was a more formal meeting of the sanhedrin, the highest court of the Jews. Luke 22 : 66–71, and parallels. This meeting was intended to confirm the results of the informal hearing in the house of Annas. But both meetings were little more than a form. The court had really decided the question beforehand; it had determined to bring Jesus by any means, lawful or otherwise, to his death. When faced by his enemies, our Lord declared plainly that he was the Messiah, the Son of God. That answer was enough to satisfy the accusers. Jesus was judged guilty of blasphemy.

Matthew 27:2-56, and Parallels

But the sanhedrin did not possess the power of life and death. Before Jesus could be executed, therefore, the findings of the sanhedrin had to be confirmed by Pilate, the Roman procurator. And at first Pilate was recalcitrant to the Jews' demands; he was not able to find in Jesus any cause of death. John 18 : 28–38, and parallels. In his perplexity, Pilate sent the prisoner to be examined by Herod Antipas, the tetrarch of Galilee, who was at the time in Jerusalem. Luke 23 : 6–12. But this hearing also was without decisive result.

At last Pilate yielded, against his better judgment, to the importunity of the Jewish leaders and the mad shouts of the crowds, who had turned now against the One whom formerly they had honored. Matt. 27 : 15–30, and parallels. Pilate delivered Jesus up to the will of the Jews. Before the execution, however, the Prisoner was cruelly scourged and mocked by the Roman soldiers. Then when a last effort of Pilate had failed to placate the wrath of Jesus' enemies, John 19 : 4–16, our Lord was finally taken out of the city to be crucified. Luke 23 : 26–33, and parallels.

The Prisoner at first was compelled to bear the cross on which he was to be put to death, but when his strength gave way a certain Simon of Cyrene was pressed into service. A crowd of people from Jerusalem followed the Prisoner, and especially a number of women who lamented. At last the place of execution was reached. It was called "Golgotha," or according to the Latin translation of the name, "Calvary." There they crucified our Lord. Matt. 27 : 33–56, and parallels.

With him were crucified two thieves, of whom one repented at the last hour, and received salvation. A number of sayings which Jesus uttered on the cross are recorded in the Gospels. At the moment of death, he cried, "It is finished." John 19 : 30. The meaning of that saying is plain. The work for which our Lord came into the world at last was done. The Lord of glory had died to wash away the sins of all believers. The just penalty of sin had been borne by the One who knew no sin.

QUESTIONS ON LESSON XII

1. Summarize the teaching of Jesus on the last evening before the crucifixion.
2. What happened in Gethsemane?
3. Describe the trial of Jesus before the sanhedrin and before Pilate.
4. Why did the Jewish leaders put Jesus to death? Why did Jesus consent to die?
5. Give an account of the crucifixion of our Lord.

LESSON XIII
The Resurrection

The death of Christ was the greatest event that history has ever seen. By that event the grace of God triumphed over sin, and a lost world was redeemed. Apart from Christ we all deserve eternal death. But the Lord of glory, on Calvary, bore the guilt which belonged to us, and made us children of God.

So great an event was accomplished without flare of heavenly trumpets or blazing of heavenly light. To many, the death of Christ seemed to be merely the execution of a criminal. But there were not wanting some strange phenomena which marked the greatness of the event. From twelve o'clock on the day of the crucifixion there was darkness until three o'clock, when Jesus died. Then the veil of the Temple was rent, there was an earthquake, and graves were opened. Thus was nature made to recognize the suffering and the triumph of her Lord.

After Jesus had died, his side was pierced by one of the soldiers whom Pilate had sent at the instance of the Jews in order that those who had been crucified should be killed and their bodies removed before the Sabbath. From the body of Jesus there came out blood and water. The event was witnessed by John the son of Zebedee, the writer of the Fourth Gospel. John 19 : 31–42.

Matthew 27:57-66

Then, in the late afternoon of the same day Joseph of Arimathea, a secret disciple of Jesus, removed our Lord's body from the cross and placed it in a new tomb. Mark 15 : 42–46, and parallels. Another secret disciple, or half-disciple, Nicodemus, came also to anoint the body. John 19 : 39. Certain women also came to see where Jesus was laid. Luke 23 : 55, 56, and parallels. The chief priests and Pharisees, on the other hand, obtained a guard from Pilate, to watch the tomb, lest the disciples of Jesus should steal the body of Jesus away and say that he had risen from the dead. Matt. 27 : 62–66.

Matthew 28:2-4, 11-15

The next day was Saturday, the Old Testament Sabbath. The friends of Jesus rested on that day. But very early on Sunday morning, the women started to the tomb bearing spices in order to anoint the body. But before they arrived, our Lord had already risen from the dead. There had been an earthquake, an angel had rolled away the stone from the sepulcher, and our Lord himself had risen. At the sight of the angel, the soldiers of the guard, in their fear, "became as dead men." Matt. 28 : 2–4. All that they could do was to report the event to the chief priests who had sent them. Vs. 11–15.

Matthew 28:1, and Parallels; John 20:2; Matthew 28:5-10, and Parallels

Then the women arrived at the tomb, and found it empty. Matt. 28 : 1, and parallels. One of them, Mary Magdalene, went back to tell Peter and John. John 20 : 2. The others remained at the tomb, and there saw two angels who announced to them that Jesus was risen from the dead. On their way back to the city Jesus himself met them, and they fell down, grasped his feet, and worshiped him. Matt. 28 : 5–10, and parallels.

John 20:3-18

Meanwhile, at the message of Mary Magdalene, Peter and John ran to the tomb, found it empty, and believed that Jesus really was risen. John 20 : 3–10. But Mary Magdalene, after they had gone, stood weeping at the tomb; she supposed that some one had taken the body of her Lord away. Then Jesus himself came to her, her sorrow was changed into joy, and she joined her voice to that of the other women who told the disciples of the glad event. Vs. 11–18.

I Corinthians 15:5; Luke 24:13-49; John 20:19-23

Thus far, Jesus himself had been seen only by the women. But now he appeared to Peter, I Cor. 15 : 5; Luke 24 : 34, and to two of the disciples who were walking to the village of Emmaus. At first the two disciples did not know him; but they recognized him at Emmaus when he broke the bread. Then, on the evening of the same Sunday, he appeared to the apostles in Jerusalem. I Cor. 15 : 5; Luke 24 : 36–49; John 20 : 19–23. All doubts were removed when he showed them the wounds in his hands and his side, and partook of food in their presence. Then he interpreted the Scriptures to them, as he had done to the two disciples on the walk to Emmaus, showing them that it was necessary that the Messiah should suffer. Finally he breathed upon them, and said, "Receive ye the Holy Spirit."

John 20:24-29

Thomas, one of the apostles, who had been absent from this meeting with the risen Lord, refused to believe at the mere word of the others. But Jesus dealt very graciously with the doubting disciple. Again, one week later, he came to the apostles, the doors of the room being shut, and presented to Thomas his hands and his side. All doubts now melted away in the joy of meeting with the risen Lord. Thomas answered and said unto him, "My Lord and my God." John 20 : 24–29.

John 21:1-24; I Corinthians 15:6; Matthew 28:16-20

The apostles then went back to Galilee in accordance with Jesus' command, and in Galilee also Jesus appeared to them. First he appeared to seven of the disciples on the shores of the Sea of Galilee. Among the seven was John the son of Zebedee, who has given an account of the event in his Gospel. John 21 : 1–24. Then there was a great appearance of Jesus on a mountain. At that time, apparently, not only the eleven apostles were present, but also five hundred other disciples. I Cor. 15 : 6; Matt. 28 : 16–20. On the mountain Jesus instituted the sacrament of baptism, and gave his disciples the Great Commission to make disciples of all nations. The execution of that commission has sometimes been attended with discouragements. But the risen Lord promised always to be with his Church.

I Corinthians 15:7; Acts 1:1-11

After the appearances in Galilee, the apostles returned to Jerusalem. It was no doubt in Jerusalem that Jesus appeared to James, his own brother, I Cor. 15 : 7, who during the earthly ministry had not believed on him. Other appearances also occurred there. At one or more of these appearances Jesus commanded the apostles to wait in Jerusalem until the Holy Spirit should come upon them. Then, said Jesus, they were to be witnesses of him "both in Jerusalem, and in all Judæa and Samaria, and unto the uttermost part of the earth." Acts 1 : 8. Finally, forty days after the resurrection, Jesus led his disciples out to the Mount of Olives, on the way to Bethany, and there he was taken from them in a cloud into heaven. The disciples were saddened and bewildered by the departure of their Lord. But their sadness was soon turned into joy. "Two men stood by them in white apparel; who also said, Ye men of Galilee, why stand ye looking into heaven?

this Jesus, who was received up from you into heaven, shall so come in like manner as ye beheld him going into heaven." Acts 1 : 10, 11. The disciples went then into the city, where they were constantly in the Temple, praising God.

QUESTIONS ON LESSON XIII

1. Describe the burial of Jesus. How long did his body rest in the tomb?
2. Enumerate the persons who saw the empty tomb.
3. Enumerate, so far as the facts are known, the persons who saw Jesus after the resurrection.
4. In what books of the New Testament are the facts about the resurrection mentioned?
5. What is the importance of the resurrection of Jesus for our Christian faith?
6. Describe the change which the resurrection produced in the early disciples of Jesus.

LESSON XIV

The Beginnings of the Christian Church

The Christian Church is founded on the fact of the resurrection of Jesus; if that fact had not occurred there would be no Church to-day. The disciples of Jesus of Nazareth were evidently far inferior to him in spiritual discernment and in courage. Evidently they could not hope to succeed if he had failed. And with his death what little strength they may have had before was utterly destroyed. In the hour of his trial they had deserted him in cowardly flight. And when he was taken from them by a shameful death, they were in despair. Never did a movement seem to be more hopelessly dead.

But then the surprising thing occurred. Those same weak, discouraged men began, in a few days, in Jerusalem, the very scene of their disgrace, a spiritual movement the like of which the world has never seen. What produced the wonderful change? What was it that transformed those weak, discouraged men into the spiritual conquerors of the world?

The answer of those men themselves was plain. Their despair, they said, gave way to triumphant joy because the Lord Jesus had risen from the dead, and because they were convinced of his resurrection by the empty tomb and by the appearances of Jesus himself. No other real explanation has yet been discovered to account for the sudden transformation of the despair of the disciples into triumphant joy. The very existence of the Christian Church itself, therefore, is the strongest testimony to the resurrection; for without the resurrection the Church could never have come into being.

Acts 1: 12-26

After the ascension of Jesus, which was studied in the last lesson, the apostles returned to Jerusalem, and obeyed the command of Jesus by waiting for the coming of the Holy Spirit. But the period of waiting was not a period of idleness; it was spent, on the contrary, in praising God and in prayer. One definite action was taken—the place of Judas, the traitor, who had killed himself in his remorse, was filled by the choice of Matthias. Acts 1 : 15–26. At that time, certain women and a number of other disciples were gathered together with the apostles, making a total of about one hundred and twenty persons. It was upon that little company of praying disciples, or rather upon the promise of Jesus which had been made to them, that the hope of the world was based.

Acts, Chapter 2

At last, at the feast of Pentecost, fifty days after the passover, the promise of Jesus was fulfilled; the Holy Spirit came upon the disciples to fit them for the evangelization of the world. Acts 2 : 1–13. They were all together in one place; there was a sound as of a rushing, mighty wind; cloven tongues, like tongues of fire, sat upon each one of them; they were all filled with the Holy Spirit, and began to speak with other languages as the Spirit gave them utterance. When the crowd came together to see the wonderful thing that had happened, Peter preached the first sermon of the Christian Church. Vs. 14–36. At the preaching of Peter three thousand persons were converted; the campaign of world conquest had begun. Vs. 37–42.

The campaign from the beginning was a campaign of witnessing, in accordance with Jesus' command. Acts 1 : 8. The Christian Church was to conquer the world, not by exhorting men to live a certain kind of life, but by bringing them a piece of news. The Son of God, said the Christian missionaries, died on the cross and then rose again. That was the good news that conquered the world. Christianity from the beginning was a way of life, but it was a way of life founded upon a piece of news, a way of life founded upon historical facts. The meaning of the facts was not revealed all at once, but it was revealed in part from the very beginning, and throughout the Apostolic Age the revelation came in greater and greater fullness, especially through the instrumentality of Paul.

The life of the Early Church in Jerusalem was in some respects like that of the Jews. The disciples continued to observe the Jewish fasts and feasts and were constantly in the Temple. But a new joy animated the company of believers. Their Lord was indeed taken from them for a time, and they did not know when he would return, but meanwhile he was present with them through his Spirit, and already he had saved them from their sins.

Even in external observances the believers were distinguished from the rest of the Jews. Entrance into their company was marked by the sacrament of baptism, which signified the washing away of sin; and their continued fellowship with one another and with the risen Lord found expression in the sacrament of the Lord's Supper, which commemorated the atoning death of Jesus. There were also common meals. And those who had property devoted it, in a purely voluntary way, to the needs of their poorer brethren. The disciples attended diligently, moreover, to the teaching of the apostles, and engaged constantly in prayer.

Acts, Chapter 3

The preaching of the apostles in Jerusalem was authenticated by miracles. One notable miracle is narrated in detail in the book of The Acts. Ch. 3. As Peter and John were going up into the Temple at the hour of prayer, they healed a lame beggar, who was in the habit of sitting at the gate. The miracle was the means of bringing to the people something better than bodily healing; for when the crowd came together in wonder at the healing of the lame man, Peter proclaimed to them the good news of the salvation which Jesus had wrought.

Acts, Chapter 4

The Sadducees, the ruling class, being incensed at such a proclamation, laid hands upon the two apostles, and brought them before the sanhedrin. Acts 4 : 1-22. But even when Peter boldly announced to them that the name of that Jesus whom they had put to death was the only name which could bring salvation to men, they were unable to do more than warn the recalcitrant preachers. A notable miracle had been wrought, and they could not deny it. When Peter and John came again to the company of believers, all the company united in a glorious prayer of praise. The answer to the prayer was plainly given. "The place was shaken wherein they were gathered together; and they were all filled with the Holy Spirit, and they spake the word of God with boldness."

QUESTIONS ON LESSON XIV

1. Show how the Christian Church is founded upon the fact of the resurrection.
2. Describe the choice of Matthias.
3. Who were gathered together in the "upper room" in Jerusalem?
4. Describe the coming of the Spirit on the Day of Pentecost.
5. Was the speaking with other tongues on the Day of Pentecost the same as the gift of tongues described in the First Epistle to the Corinthians? If not, what was the difference?
6. Why were the Sadducees opposed to the preaching of Peter and John?

LESSON XV

The First Persecution

Acts 5:1-11

The life of the early Jerusalem church was full of a holy joy. But even in those first glorious days the Church had to battle against sin, and not all of those who desired to join themselves to the disciples were of true Christian life. One terrible judgment of God was inflicted in order to preserve the purity of the Church. Acts 5 : 1–11.

A certain Ananias, with Sapphira his wife, had sold a possession, in accordance with the custom of those early days, and had laid part of the price at the apostles' feet that it might be distributed to the poorer disciples. Part of the price was withheld, and yet Ananias and his wife pretended to have given all. Ananias was not required to sell his field, or to give all of the price after he had sold it. His sin was the sin of deceit. He had lied to the Holy Spirit. Terrible was the judgment of God; Ananias and Sapphira were stricken down dead, and great fear came upon all who heard.

Acts 5:12-42

The apostles and the Church enjoyed the favor of the people—
a favor which was mingled with awe. Many miracles were wrought
by the apostles; multitudes of sick people were brought to be healed.
But the Sadducees made another attempt to put a stop to the dangerous movement. Acts 5 : 17–42. They laid hands upon all the apostles,
as they had laid hands upon two of them once before, and put them
all in prison. But in the night the apostles were released by an angel
of the Lord, and at once, in obedience to the angel's command, went
and taught boldly in the Temple. When they were arrested again,
Peter said simply, "We must obey God rather than men. The Jesus
whom you slew has been raised up by God as a Prince and a Saviour,
and we are witnesses of these things and so is the Holy Spirit." Vs.
29–32, in substance. It was a bold answer, and the sanhedrin was
incensed. But Gamaliel, a Pharisee, one of the most noted of the
Jewish teachers, advocated a policy of watchful waiting. If the new
movement were of God, he said, there was no use in fighting against
it; if it were of men it would fail of itself as other Messianic movements had failed. The cautious policy prevailed, so far as any attempt
at inflicting the death penalty was concerned. But the apostles before
they were released were scourged. The suffering and shame did not
prevent their preaching. They rejoiced that they were counted worthy
to suffer dishonor for the name of Jesus.

Acts 6:1-6

The early Jerusalem church was composed partly of Aramaic-
speaking Jews who had always lived in Palestine, and partly of Greek-
speaking Jews who were connected with the Judaism of the Dispersion.
The latter class murmured because their widows were neglected in
the daily ministrations. In order that the matter might be attended
to without turning the apostles aside from their work of teaching
and preaching, seven men were chosen to preside over the distribution
of help to the needy members of the church. Acts 6 : 1–6. But these
seven were no mere "business men." They were "full of the Spirit
and of wisdom," and at least two of them became prominent in the
preaching of the gospel.

Acts 6:7 to 8:3

One of these two was Stephen, a "man full of faith and cf the Holy
Spirit." Stephen "wrought great wonders and signs among the people,"

and also preached in the synagogues which were attended by certain of the Greek-speaking Jews residing at Jerusalem. By his preaching he stirred up opposition. And the opposition was of a new kind. Up to that time the objection to the Early Church had come, principally at least, from the Sadducees. But the Sadducees were a worldly aristocracy, out of touch with the masses of the people, and in their efforts against the Church they had been checked again and again by the popular favor which the disciples of Jesus enjoyed. Now, however, that popular favor began to wane. It became evident that although the disciples continued to observe the Jewish fasts and feasts, their preaching really meant the beginning of a new era. The people were not ready for such a change, and especially the leaders of the people, the Pharisees, who, since the crucifixion of Jesus, had shown no persecuting zeal, came out in active opposition.

The result was at once evident. Stephen was arrested, and was charged with revolutionary teaching about the Temple. The charge was false; Stephen did not say that the Temple worship should then and there be abandoned by the disciples of Jesus. But he did proclaim the beginning of a new era, and the presence, in the person of Jesus, of one greater than Moses. So, after a great and bold speech of Stephen, he was hurried out of the city and stoned. As Stephen was stoned, he called on Jesus, saying, "Lord Jesus, receive my spirit," and then kneeling down he prayed for forgiveness of his enemies: "Lord, lay not this sin to their charge." Acts 6 : 8 to 8 : 3

Thus died the first Christian martyr. The Greek word "martyr" means "witness." Others had witnessed to the saving work of Christ by their words; Stephen now witnessed also by his death.

When Stephen was stoned, the witnesses had laid "their garments at the feet of a young man named Saul." Saul was to become the greatest preacher of the faith which then he laid waste. But meanwhile he was a leader in a great persecution.

The persecution scattered the disciples far and wide from Jerusalem, though the apostles remained. But this scattering resulted only in the wider spread of the gospel. Everywhere they went the persecuted disciples proclaimed the faith for which they suffered. Thus the very rage of the enemies was an instrument in God's hand for bringing the good news of salvation to the wide world.

Acts 8:4-40

Among those who were scattered abroad by the persecution was Philip, one of the seven men who had been appointed to care for the ministration to the poor. This Philip, who is called "the evangelist," to distinguish him from the apostle of the same name, went to Samaria, and preached to the Samaritans. It was a step on the way toward a Gentile mission, but the Samaritans themselves were not Gentiles but half-Jews. When the apostles at Jerusalem heard of the work of Philip, they sent Peter and John from among their own number, and through Peter and John the Samaritans received special manifestations of the Holy Spirit. Acts 8 : 4–25. Then Philip went to a desert road leading from Jerusalem to Gaza. There he preached the gospel to an Ethiopian treasurer, who despite his employment in a foreign country may have been of Jewish descent. Vs. 26–40. Yet the preaching to him was another preparation for the spread of the gospel out into the Gentile world.

QUESTIONS ON LESSON XV

1. What was the sin of Ananias and Sapphira? Was the relief of the needy in the early Jerusalem church what is now called communism or socialism? If not, why not?
2. What was the fundamental difference between the two first imprisonments of apostles in Jerusalem, and the persecution which began with the martyrdom of Stephen? Why was the latter more serious?
3. Outline the speech of Stephen.
4. Describe the progress of the gospel in Samaria.

LESSON XVI

The Conversion of Paul

The work of the Early Church was at first carried on only among the Jews. The Lord Jesus, it is true, had commanded the apostles to make disciples of all the nations, but he had not made it perfectly plain when the Gentile work should begin, or on what terms the Gentiles should be received. Conceivably, therefore, the early disciples might have thought it might be the will of God that all Israel should first be evangelized before the gospel should be brought to the other nations; and conceivably also the men of the other nations, when they finally should receive the gospel, might be required to unite themselves with the people of Israel and keep the Mosaic Law. The guidance of the Holy Spirit was required, therefore, before the gospel should be offered freely to Gentiles without requiring them to become Jews.

But that guidance, in God's good time, was plainly and gloriously given.

One of the most important steps in the preparation for the Gentile mission was the calling of a leader. And the leader whom God called was one upon whom human choice never would have rested; for the chosen leader was none other than Saul, the bitterest enemy of the Church.

Saul, whose Roman name was Paul, was born at Tarsus, a center of Greek culture, and the chief city of Cilicia, the coast country in the southeastern part of Asia Minor, near the northeastern corner of the Mediterranean Sea. In Tarsus the family of Paul belonged by no means to the humblest of the population, for Paul's father and then Paul himself possessed Roman citizenship, which in the provinces of the empire was a highly prized privilege possessed only by a few. Thus by birth in a Greek university city and by possession of Roman citizenship Paul was connected with the life of the Gentile world. Such connection was not without importance for his future service as apostle to the Gentiles.

Far more important, however, was the Jewish element in his preparation. Although Paul no doubt spoke Greek in childhood, he also in childhood spoke Aramaic, the language of Palestine, and his family regarded themselves as being in spirit Jews of Palestine rather than of the Dispersion, Aramaic-speaking Jews rather than Greek-speaking Jews, "Hebrews" rather than "Hellenists." Both in Tarsus and in Jerusalem, moreover, Paul was brought up in the strictest sect of the Pharisees. Thus despite his birth in a Gentile city, Paul was not a "liberal Jew"; he was not inclined to break down the separation between Jews and Gentiles, or relax the strict requirements of the Mosaic Law. On the contrary, his zeal for the Law went beyond that of many of his contemporaries. The fact is of enormous importance for the understanding of Paul's gospel; for Paul's gospel of justification by faith is based not upon a lax interpretation of the law of God, but upon a strict interpretation. Only, according to that gospel,

Christ has paid the penalty of the law once for all on the cross. According to Paul, it is because the full penalty of the law has been paid, and not at all because the law is to be taken lightly, that the Christian is free from the law.

Acts 9:1-19, and Parallels

Early in life Paul went to Jerusalem, to receive training under Gamaliel, the famous Pharisaic teacher. And in Jerusalem, when he had still not reached middle age, he engaged bitterly in persecution of the Church. He was filled with horror at a blasphemous sect that proclaimed a crucified malefactor to be the promised King of Israel, and that tended, perhaps, to break down the permanent significance of the law. It is a great mistake to suppose that before he was converted Paul was gradually getting nearer to Christianity. On the contrary, he was if anything getting further away, and it was while he was on a mad persecuting expedition that his conversion finally occurred.

The conversion of Paul was different in one important respect from the conversion of ordinary Christians. Ordinary Christians, like Paul, are converted by the Holy Spirit, who is the Spirit of Jesus. But in the case of ordinary Christians human instruments are used—the preaching of the gospel, or godly parents, or the like. In the case of Paul, on the other hand, no such instrument was used, but the Lord Jesus himself appeared to Paul and brought him the gospel. Paul himself says in one of his Epistles that he saw the Lord. I Cor. 9:1; 15:8. It was that fact which made Paul, unlike ordinary Christians, but like Peter and the other apostles, an actual eyewitness to the resurrection of Christ.

A wonderful thing, moreover, was the way in which Jesus appeared to Paul. He might naturally have appeared to him in anger, to condemn him for the persecution of the Church. Instead he appeared in love, to receive him into fellowship and to make him the greatest of the apostles. That was grace—pure grace, pure undeserved favor. It is always a matter of pure grace when a man is saved by the Lord Jesus, but in the case of Paul, the persecutor, the grace was wonderfully plain. Paul never forgot that grace of Christ; he never hated anything so much as the thought that a man can be saved by his own good works, or his own character, or his own obedience to God's commands. The gospel of Paul is a proclamation of the grace of God.

Paul saw the Lord on the road to Damascus, where he had been intending to persecute the Church. Acts 9 : 1-19, and parallels. As he was nearing the city, suddenly at midday a bright light shone around him above the brightness of the sun. Those who accompanied him remained speechless, seeing the light but not distinguishing the person, hearing a sound, but not distinguishing the words. Paul, on the other hand, saw the Lord Jesus and listened to what Jesus said. Then, at the command of Jesus, he went into Damascus. For three days he was blind, then received his sight through the ministrations of Ananias, an otherwise unknown disciple, and was baptized. Then he proceeded to labor for the Lord by whom he had been saved.

· Soon, however, he went away for a time into Arabia. Gal. 1 : 17. It is not known how far the journey took him or how long it lasted, except that it lasted less than three years. Nothing is said, in the New Testament, moreover, about what Paul did in Arabia. But even if he engaged in missionary preaching, he also meditated on the great thing that God had done for him; and certainly he prayed.

QUESTIONS ON LESSON XVI

1. Where was Paul born? Find the place on a map. What sort of city was it.
2. What is known about Paul's boyhood home, and about his education? In what books of the New Testament is the information given?
3. Why did Paul persecute the Church?
4. Describe in detail what the book of The Acts says about the conversion of Paul. Where does Paul mention the conversion in his Epistles?
5. How did the conversion of Paul differ from the conversion of an ordinary Christian? In what particulars was it like the conversion of an ordinary Christian?
6. What did Paul do after the conversion?

LESSON XVII
The Gospel Given to the Gentiles

Saul of Tarsus was not only converted directly by the Lord Jesus; he was also called just as directly by Jesus to be an apostle, and especially an apostle to the Gentiles. But other instruments were also used in the beginning of the Gentile mission. Even Peter, whose work continued for a number of years afterwards to be chiefly among the Jews, was led by the Holy Spirit to take a notable step in the offering of the gospel freely to the whole world.

Acts 9:31-43

During the period of peace which followed after the persecution at the time of the death of Stephen, Peter went down to labor in the coastal plain of Palestine. Acts 9 : 31–43. At Lydda he healed a lame man, Æneas; at Joppa, on the coast, he raised Dorcas from the dead. And it was at Joppa that he received the guidance of the Holy Spirit as to the reception of Gentiles into the Church. Ch. 10.

Acts, Chapter 10

At midday Peter went up upon the flat housetop to pray. There he fell into a trance, and saw a vessel like a great sheet let down from heaven, and in it all kinds of animals which it was forbidden in the Mosaic Law to use for food. A voice came to him: "Rise, Peter; kill and eat. But Peter said, Not so, Lord; for I have never eaten anything that is common and unclean. And a voice came unto him again the second time, What God hath cleansed, make not thou common. And this was done thrice: and straightway the vessel was received up into heaven."

The meaning of this vision was soon made plain. A Roman officer, Cornelius, a devout Gentile, living at Cæsarea, which was a seaport about thirty miles north of Joppa, had been commanded in a vision to send for Peter. The messengers of Cornelius arrived at Peter's house just after Peter's vision was over. The Holy Spirit commanded Peter to go with them. Arriving at Cæsarea, the apostle went into the house where Cornelius and his friends were assembled, and there proclaimed to them the gospel of the Lord Jesus. While he was still speaking, the Holy Spirit fell upon all those who were present, upon the Gentiles as well as upon the Jews. Then said Peter, "Can any man forbid the water, that these should not be baptized, who have received the Holy Spirit as well as we?" So the Gentiles were baptized.

A very important step had been taken. Cornelius, it is true, was a "God-fearer"—that is, he belonged to the class of Gentiles frequently mentioned in the book of The Acts who worshiped the God of Israel and were friendly to the Jews. Nevertheless, he was still outside the covenant people, and under the old dispensation he could not be received into covenant privileges until he united himself with the nation by submitting himself to the whole Mosaic Law. Yet now such restrictions were removed by the plain guidance of the Spirit of God. Evidently an entirely new dispensation had begun.

Acts 11:1-18

At Jerusalem Peter's strange action in receiving Gentiles into the Church without requiring them to become Jews gave rise to some discussion. Acts 11 : 1–18. But the apostles had no difficulty in convincing the brethren of the necessity for what he had done. The guidance of the Holy Spirit had been perfectly plain. When the brethren heard what Peter said, "they held their peace, and glorified God, saying, Then to the Gentiles also hath God granted repentance unto life."

The freedom of the Gentiles had not yet, however, fully been revealed. For a time the case of Cornelius seems to have been regarded as exceptional. The Holy Spirit had plainly commanded Peter to receive Cornelius and his friends without requiring them to be united to the people of Israel, but perhaps similar definite guidance was required before others could be received. The underlying reason for Gentile freedom, in other words, had not yet fully been revealed.

The revelation, however, was not long delayed; it came especially through the Apostle Paul. But meanwhile Paul was being prepared for his work.

Acts 9: 19-30, and Parallels

After the journey to Arabia, which was mentioned at the end of Lesson XVI, Paul returned to Damascus, and preached to the Jews, endeavoring to convince them that Jesus was really the Messiah. His preaching aroused opposition, and the Jews, with the help of an officer of King Aretas of Arabia, had tried to kill him. But the brethren lowered him over the city wall in a basket, and so he escaped to Jerusalem, Acts 9 : 23–25; II Cor. 11 : 31–33, where he desired to become acquainted with Peter. No doubt he then talked with Peter especially about the events of the earthly ministry of Jesus and the appearances of the risen Christ. He also engaged in preaching to the Greek-speaking Jews. But when these Greek-speaking Jews sought to kill him, the brethren sent him away to Tarsus. He was unwilling to go, being desirous of repairing the harm which he had done to the church at Jerusalem; but a definite command of the Lord Jesus sent him now forth to the country of the Gentiles. Acts 9 : 26–30; 22 : 17–21; Gal. 1 : 18–24. He labored in or near Tarsus, preaching the faith which formerly he had laid waste.

Acts 11:19-26

Meanwhile an important new step in the progress of the gospel into the Gentile world was taken at Antioch. Acts 11 : 19–26. Antioch, the capital of the Roman province of Syria, was situated on the Orontes River, near the northeastern corner of the Mediterranean Sea. It was the third greatest city of the empire, ranking immediately after Rome and Alexandria. And among the great Gentile cities it was the first which was encountered on the march of the gospel out from Jerusalem to the conquest of the world.

At Antioch, certain unnamed Jews of Cyprus and Cyrene, who had been scattered from Jerusalem by the persecution at the time of Stephen's death, took the important step of preaching the word of God to the Gentiles. Before, they had spoken only to Jews; here they spoke also to the Gentiles. Gentiles were received no longer merely in isolated cases like the case of Cornelius, but in large numbers. To investigate what had happened, Barnabas, an honorable member of the early Jerusalem church, Acts 4 : 36, 37, was sent from Jerusalem to Antioch. Barnabas at once recognized the hand of God, and sent to Tarsus to seek Paul. He and Paul then labored abundantly in the Antioch church. At Antioch the disciples of Jesus were first called "Christians"—no doubt by the Gentile population of the city. The fact is not unimportant. It shows that even outsiders had come to see that the Christian Church was something distinct from Judaism. A distinct name had come to be required.

QUESTIONS ON LESSON XVII

1. Describe the conversion of Cornelius in detail. What was the importance of the event?
2. What was the meaning of Peter's vision on the housetop at Joppa?
3. What important step was taken at Antioch?
4. Trace the part of Barnabas in furthering the work of Paul.
5. Show how every successive step in the offering of the gospel to the Gentiles was taken under the guidance of the Holy Spirit.

LESSON XVIII
The First Missionary Journey and the Apostolic Council

Acts 11:27 to 12:25

After a time of rapid growth in the Antioch church, a prophet, Agabus by name, came down from Jerusalem and prophesied a famine. The disciples determined to send relief to their brethren in Jerusalem. This they did by the instrumentality of Barnabas and Paul. Acts 11 : 27-30.

Meanwhile the Jerusalem church had been suffering renewed persecution under Herod Agrippa I, who, as a vassal of Rome, ruled over all Palestine from A.D. 41 to 44. James the son of Zebedee, one of the apostles, had been put to death, and Peter had escaped only by a wonderful interposition of God, Acts, ch. 12.

Acts, Chapters 13, 14

After Barnabas and Paul had returned to Antioch from their labor of love in Jerusalem, they were sent out, under the guidance of the Holy Spirit, upon a mission to the Gentiles, which is called the first missionary journey. Acts, chs. 13, 14. This missionary journey led first through the island of Cyprus, then, by way of Perga in Pamphylia to Pisidian Antioch on the central plateau of Asia Minor.

At Pisidian Antioch, as regularly in the cities that he visited, Paul entered first into the synagogue. In accordance with the liberal Jewish custom of that day, he was given opportunity to speak, as a visiting teacher. The congregation was composed not only of Jews but also of Gentiles who had become interested in the God of Israel and in the lofty morality of the Old Testament without definitely uniting themselves with the people of Israel—the class of persons who are called in the book of The Acts "they that feared God" or the like. These "God-fearers" constituted a picked audience; they were just the Gentiles who were most apt to be won by the new preaching, because in their case much of the preliminary instruction had been given. But the Jews themselves, at Pisidian Antioch as well as elsewhere, were jealous of the new mission to the Gentiles, which was proving so much more successful than their own. Paul and Barnabas, therefore, were obliged to give up the work in the synagogue and address themselves directly to the Gentile population. So it happened very frequently in the cities that Paul visited—at first he preached to both Jews and Gentiles in the synagogues, and then when the Jews drove him out he was obliged to preach to the Gentiles only.

Being driven out of Pisidian Antioch by a persecution instigated by the Jews, Paul and Barnabas went to Iconium, Lystra, and Derbe, which, with Pisidian Antioch, were in the southern part of the great Roman province Galatia, but not in Galatia proper, which lay farther to the north. Then, turning back from Derbe, the missionaries revisited Lystra, Iconium, and Pisidian Antioch, strengthening the disciples and appointing elders; and then returned to the church at Syrian Antioch from which the Holy Spirit had sent them forth.

The Epistle of James

During the progress of the Antioch church and of the mission which had proceeded from it, the church at Jerusalem had not been idle. At the head of it stood James, the brother of Jesus, who was not one of the twelve apostles and apparently during the earthly ministry of Jesus had not been a believer, but who had witnessed an appearance of the risen Lord. James was apparently attached permanently to the church at Jerusalem, while the Twelve engaged frequently in missionary work elsewhere. From this James there has been preserved in the New Testament a letter, The Epistle of James, which is addressed "to the twelve tribes which are of the Dispersion." This letter was written at an early time, perhaps at about the time of the first missionary journey of Paul. In the letter, James lays stress upon the high moral standard which ought to prevail in the Christian life, and he has sometimes been regarded as an advocate of "works." But this judgment should not be misunderstood. The "works" of which James is speaking are not works which are to be put alongside of faith as one of the means by which salvation is to be obtained; they are, on the contrary, works which proceed from faith and show that faith is true faith. James does not, therefore, deny the doctrine of justification by faith alone. Only he insists that true faith always results in good works. Paul meant exactly the same thing when he spoke of "faith working through love." Gal. 5 : 6. Paul and James use somewhat different language, but they mean the same thing. Faith, according to both of them, involves receiving the power of God, which then results in a life of loving service.

Acts 15:1-35; Galatians 2:1-10

The wonderful success of the first missionary journey of Paul and Barnabas caused great joy to the Antioch church. But the joy was soon marred by certain persons, commonly called "Judaizers," who came down to Antioch from Jerusalem and said that unless the Gentile converts kept the Law of Moses they could not be saved. The demand was directly contrary to the great principle of justification by faith alone; for it made salvation depend partly upon human merit. The entire life of the Church was in danger. But Paul, guided by a revelation from God, determined to comply with the wishes of the brethren at Antioch by going up to Jerusalem with Barnabas and certain others, in order to confer with the leaders of the Jerusalem church. Paul did not need any authorization from those leaders, for he had been commissioned directly by Christ; nor did he need to learn from them anything about the principles of the gospel, for the gospel had come to him through direct revelation. But he did desire to receive from the Jerusalem leaders, to whom the Judaizers falsely appealed, some such public pronouncement as would put the Judaizers clearly in the wrong and so stop their ruination of the Church's work.

The conference resulted exactly as Paul desired. Acts 15 : 1-35; Gal. 2 : 1-10. The Jerusalem leaders—James, the brother of the Lord, Peter, and John the son of Zebedee—recognized that they had absolutely nothing to add to the gospel of Paul, because he had been commissioned by Christ as truly and as directly as the original Twelve. Joyfully, therefore, they gave to Paul and Barnabas the right hand of fellowship. God had worked for Paul among the Gentiles as truly as he had worked for Peter among the Jews. With regard to the propaganda of the Judaizers, the Jerusalem church, after speeches by James and Peter presenting the same view as the view of Paul, sent a letter to the Gentile Christians in Antioch and Syria and Cilicia declaring them to be absolutely free from the Mosaic Law as a means of salvation, and directing them to refrain, out of loving regard for the Jews in the several cities, from certain things in the Gentile manner of life which were most abhorrent to Jewish feeling.

Such was the result of the "Apostolic Council," which took place at about A.D. 49. It was a great victory for the Gentile mission and for Paul, for it established clearly the unity of all the apostles under the guidance of the Holy Spirit. No wonder the church at Antioch rejoiced when the letter of the Jerusalem church was read.

QUESTIONS ON LESSON XVIII

1. Describe in detail the release of Peter from prison in the closing days of the reign of Herod Agrippa I.
2. Enumerate the visits of Paul to Jerusalem which have been studied so far.
3. What happened, on the first missionary journey, at Paphos? at Perga? at Pisidian Antioch? at Lystra?
4. Describe the Apostolic Council in detail. What was the meaning of the letter which was sent out from the council?

LESSON XIX

The Second Missionary Journey

The Apostolic Council, which was studied in the last lesson, was an important step in the progress of Christian liberty. By it the Judaizers were definitely repudiated, and salvation was based upon faith alone apart from the works of the law. But many practical difficulties still remained to be solved.

Galatians 2:11-21 ·

One such difficulty appeared at Antioch soon after the council. Gal. 2 : 11-21. The council had established the freedom of the Gentile Christians from the Mosaic Law, but it had not been determined that the Jewish Christians should give up the Law. No doubt the Jewish Christians were inwardly free from the Law; they depended for their salvation not at all upon their obedience to God's commands as set forth in the Law of Moses, but simply and solely upon the saving work of Christ accepted by faith. But so far as had yet been revealed, it might conceivably be the will of God that they should still maintain their connection with Israel by observing the whole of the Law including even its ceremonial requirements. In order, however, that the ceremonial requirements of the Law might be observed, the Jews had always been accustomed to avoid table companionship with Gentiles. What should be done, therefore, in churches like the church at Antioch, which were composed both of Jewish Christians and of Gentile Christians? How could the Jewish Christians in such churches continue to observe the ceremonial law, and still hold table companionship with their Gentile brethren?

This question faced the apostle Peter on a visit which he made to Antioch after the Apostolic Council. At first he answered the question in the interests of Gentile freedom; he allowed the unity of the Church to take precedence over the devotion of Jewish Christians to the ceremonial law. He held table companionship, therefore, with the Gentile Christians, and he did so out of true conviction with regard to the new Christian freedom. But when certain men came to Antioch from James, Peter was afraid to be seen transgressing the ceremonial law, and so began to withdraw himself from table companionship with his Gentile brethren.

Peter's action, because of its inconsistency, endangered the very life of the Church. Peter had given up the keeping of the ceremonial law in order to hold table companionship with the Gentile Christians. Then he had undertaken the keeping of the ceremonial law again. Might not the Gentile Christians be tempted to do the same thing, in order to preserve their fellowship with the greatest of the original apostles? But if the Gentile Christians should begin to keep the ceremonial law, they could not fail to think that the keeping of the ceremonial law was somehow necessary to salvation. And so the fundamental principle of Christianity—the principle of salvation by Christ alone apart from human merit—would be given up. The danger was imminent.

But God had raised up a man to fight the battle of the Church. Absolutely regardless of personal considerations, devoted solely to the truth, the Apostle Paul withstood Peter before the whole Church. It is exceedingly important to observe that Paul did not differ from Peter in principle; he differed from him only in practice. He said to Peter in effect, "You and I are quite agreed about the principle of justification by faith alone; why, therefore, do you belie your principles by your conduct?" In the very act of condemning the practice of Peter, therefore, Paul commends his principles; about the principles of the gospel the two chief apostles were fully agreed. Undoubtedly Peter was convinced by what Paul said; there was no permanent disagreement, even about matters of practice, between Peter and Paul. Thus did the Spirit of God guide and protect the Church.

Acts 15: 36 to 18: 22

Soon afterward Paul went forth from Antioch on his "second missionary journey," Acts 15 : 36 to 18 : 22. Journeying with Silas by the land route to Derbe and to Lystra, where Timothy became his associate, he then apparently went to Iconium and Pisidian Antioch and then northward into Galatia proper, that is "Galatia" in the older and narrower sense of the term. Finally he went down to Troas, a seaport on the Ægean Sea. At Troas he must have been joined by Luke, the author of The Acts, since the narrative in Acts here begins to be carried on by the use of the first person, "we," instead of "they," thus showing that the author was present.

Setting sail from Troas, the apostolic company soon came to Philippi in Macedonia, where an important church was founded. At last Paul and Silas were imprisoned, and although they were released through divine interposition and by the second thought of the city authorities, they were requested by the authorities to leave the city.

Arriving at Thessalonica, Paul preached in the synagogue, and founded an important church, chiefly composed of Gentiles. But after a stay shorter than had been intended, persecution instigated by the Jews drove Paul out of the city. He went then to Athens, where he preached not merely in the synagogue but also directly to the Gentile passers-by in the market place.

At Corinth, the capital of the Roman province Achaia, embracing Greece proper, large numbers of converts were won, and Paul spent about two years in the city. Not long after the beginning of this Corinthian residence, he wrote the two Thessalonian Epistles.

The First and Second Epistles
to the Thessalonians

The First Epistle to the Thessalonians was written just after Paul had received his first news from the Thessalonian church. He had been obliged to leave Thessalonica before he had intended. Would his work in that city be permanent? Would the converts remain faithful to Christ? These were serious questions. The Thessalonian converts were living in the midst of a corrupt paganism, and Paul had not had time to instruct them fully in the things of Christ. Every human probability was against the maintenance of their Christian life. But at last Paul received his first news from Thessalonica. And the news was good news. God was watching over his children; the great wonder had been wrought; a true Christian church had been founded at Thessalonica. The letter which Paul wrote at such a time is very naturally a simple, warm expression of gratitude to God.

At the same time, in the letter, Paul comforts the Thessalonians in view of the death of certain of their number, gives instruction about the second coming of Christ, and urges the converts to live a diligent and orderly life.

The Second Epistle to the Thessalonians was written very soon after the former Epistle. It reiterates the teaching of I Thessalonians, with correction of a misunderstanding which had crept into the church with regard to the second coming of Christ.

QUESTIONS ON LESSON XIX

1. What practical question arose at Antioch after the Apostolic Council?
2. How did Paul show the agreement in principle between himself and Peter?
3. What was the inconsistency of Peter's action? Did Paul necessarily condemn Jewish Christians who continued to observe the ceremonial law? What principle was at stake at Antioch? What does Paul in his Epistles say about Peter after this time? Was there any permanent disagreement?
4. Why did Paul separate from Barnabas at the beginning of the second missionary journey? What does Paul say afterwards about Barnabas? Was there any permanent disagreement between Paul and Barnabas or between Paul and Mark?
5. Describe what happened at Troas, Philippi, Thessalonica, Berea, Athens, Corinth.
6. What was the occasion for the writing of I Thessalonians? of II Thessalonians?

LESSON XX

The Third Missionary Journey. The Epistle to the Galatians

At Corinth, on the second missionary journey, the Jews made charges before the Roman proconsul Gallio against Paul. But Gallio dismissed the charges as concerning only the Jewish Law. It was an important decision. Judaism was tolerated in the Roman Empire, and if Christianity was regarded as a variety of Judaism it would be tolerated too. Such was usually the practice of the Roman authorities in the very early days; the Roman authorities often protected the Christian missionaries against the Jews.

Finally leaving Corinth, Paul went by way of Ephesus, where he made only a brief stay, to Palestine and then back to Syrian Antioch.

Acts 18:23 to 21:15

After having spent some time at Syrian Antioch, he started out on his third missionary journey. Acts 18 : 23 to 21 : 15. First he went through Asia Minor to Ephesus, apparently passing through Galatia proper on his way. At Ephesus he spent about three years.

The Epistle to the Galatians

It was probably during this Ephesian residence that Paul wrote the Epistle to the Galatians; and probably "the churches of Galatia" to which the Epistle is addressed were churches in Galatia proper in the northern part of the great Roman province Galatia. Another view regards the Epistle as being addressed to the well-known churches at Pisidian Antioch, Iconium, Lystra, and Derbe, which were in the southern part of the Roman province. When this view is adopted, the writing of the Epistle is usually put at a somewhat earlier time in the life of Paul.

The occasion for the writing of the Epistle to the Galatians can easily be discovered on the basis of the letter itself. After Paul had left Galatia, certain other teachers had come into the country. These teachers were men of the Jewish race, and they are usually called "Judaizers." What they taught can be established fairly well on the basis of Paul's answer to them. They agreed with Paul in believing that Jesus was truly the Messiah, and that he had risen from the dead. Apparently they had no objection to Paul's doctrine of the deity of Christ, and they agreed, apparently, that faith in Christ is necessary to salvation. But they maintained that something else is also necessary to salvation—namely, union with the nation of Israel and the keeping of the Mosaic Law. The Judaizers, then, maintained that a man is saved by faith and works; whereas Paul maintained that a man is saved by faith alone.

The Galatian Christians had been impressed by what the Judaizers had said. Already they had begun to observe some of the Jewish fasts and feasts. And they were on the point of taking the decisive step of uniting themselves definitely with the people of Israel and undertaking the observance of the Mosaic Law. It was to keep them from taking that decisive step that Paul wrote the Epistle. At first sight the question at issue might seem to have little importance to-day. No one in the Church nowadays is in danger of uniting himself with Israel or undertaking to keep the ceremonial law. If Paul had treated the question in Galatia in a merely practical way, his letter would be of no value to us. But as a matter of fact Paul did not treat the question in a merely practical way; he treated it as a question of principle. He saw clearly that what was really endangered by the propaganda of the Judaizers was the great principle of grace; the true question was whether salvation is to be earned partly by what man can do or whether it is an absolutely free gift of God.

That question is just as important in the modern Church as it was in Galatia in the first century. There are many in the modern Church who maintain that salvation is obtained by character, or by men's own obedience to the commands of Christ, or by men's own acceptance of Christ's ideal of life. These are the modern Judaizers. And the Epistle to the Galatians is directed against them just as much as it was directed against the Judaizers of long ago.

Paul refuted the Judaizers by establishing the meaning of the cross of Christ. Salvation, he said, was obtained simply and solely by what Christ did when he died for the sins of believers. The curse of God's law, said Paul, rests justly upon all men, for all men have sinned. That curse of the law brings the penalty of death. But the Lord Jesus, the eternal Son of God, took the penalty upon himself by dying instead of us. We therefore go free.

Such is the gospel of Jesus Christ as preached by Paul, and as defended in the Epistle to the Galatians. That gospel, Paul said, is received by faith. Faith is not a meritorious act; it simply means accepting what Christ has done. It cannot be mingled with an appeal to human merit. Christ will do everything or nothing. Either accept as a free gift what Christ has done, or else earn salvation by perfect obedience. The latter alternative is impossible because of sin; the former, therefore, alone can make a man right with God.

But acceptance of the saving work of Christ means more than salvation from the guilt of sin; it means more than a fresh start in God's favor. It means also salvation from the power of sin. All men, according to Paul, are dead in sin. Salvation, then, can come only by a new creation, as Paul calls it, or, as it is called elsewhere in the New

Testament, a new birth. That new creation is wrought by the saving work of Christ, and applied by the Holy Spirit. And after the new creation has been wrought, there is a new life on the basis of it. In the new life there is still a battle against sin. But the Christian has received a new power, the power of the Holy Spirit. And when he yields himself to that new power, he fulfills in its deepest import the law of God. Only he fulfills it not by obedience in his own strength to a law which is outside of him, but by yielding to a power which God has placed in his heart. This new fulfillment of the law on the part of Christians is what Paul means when he speaks of "faith working through love"; for love involves the fulfillment of the whole law.

Such was the gospel of Paul as it is set forth in the Epistle to the Galatians. Paul had received it from the Lord Jesus Christ. Without it the Church is dead. It need not be put in long words, but it must be proclaimed without the slightest concession to human pride, if the Church is to be faithful to the Saviour who died. We deserved eternal death; the Lord Jesus, because he loved us, died in our stead. —there is the heart and core of Christianity.

QUESTIONS ON LESSON XX

1. Describe Paul's first visit to Corinth.
2. Where did Paul go at the beginning of the third missionary journey?
3. What was the occasion for the writing of the Epistle to the Galatians?
4. What great principle is defended in the Epistle? What is the meaning of the death of Christ? What is the meaning of "justification by faith"?
5. Give an outline of the Epistle, showing the three great divisions.
6. Why does Paul give, in the first part of the Epistle, a review of certain facts in his life?

LESSON XXI

The Third Missionary Journey. The Epistles to the Corinthians and to the Romans

Another Epistle, in addition to the Epistle to the Galatians, was written by Paul at Ephesus on the third missionary journey. This was the First Epistle to the Corinthians.

The First Epistle to the Corinthians

In I Corinthians, the details of congregational life are more fully discussed than in any other of the Epistles of Paul. Paul had received information about the Corinthian church partly through what was said by the "household of Chloe," who had come to Ephesus from Corinth, and partly by a letter which the Corinthian church had written. The information was not all of a favorable character. In Corinth, a Christian church was in deadly battle with paganism—paganism in thought and paganism in life. But that battle was fought to a victorious conclusion, through the guidance of an inspired apostle, and through the Holy Spirit of God in the hearts of believers.

First Paul dealt in his letter with the parties in the Corinthian church. The Corinthian Christians were in the habit of saying, "I am of Paul; and I of Apollos; and I of Cephas; and I of Christ," I Cor. 1 : 12; they seem to have been more interested in the particular form in which the gospel message was delivered than in the message itself. Paul treated the subject in a grand and lofty way. The party spirit in Corinth was merely one manifestation of intellectual pride. In reply, the apostle directed his readers to the true wisdom. And if you would possess that wisdom, he said, give up your quarreling and give up your pride.

Then there was gross sin to be dealt with, and a certain lordly indifference to moral purity. In reply, Paul pointed to the true moral implications of the gospel, and to the law of love which sometimes, as in Paul's own case, causes a Christian man to give up even privileges which might be his by right.

In chs. 12 to 14 of the Epistle, Paul dealt with the supernatural gifts of the Spirit, such as prophecy and speaking with tongues. These gifts were not continued after the Apostolic Age. But it is important for us to know about them, and the principles which Paul used in dealing with them are of permanent validity. The greatest principle was the principle of love. It is in connection with the question of gifts of the Spirit that Paul wrote his wonderful hymn about Christian love. Ch. 13.

Paganism of thought was creeping into the Corinthian church in connection with the doctrine of the resurrection. Paul dealt with this question by appealing to the plain historical evidence for the resurrection of Christ. That fact itself had not been denied in Corinth. It was supported by the testimony not only of Paul himself, but also of Peter, of the apostles, and of five hundred brethren most of whom were still alive. Paul had received the account of the death, the burial, the resurrection, and the appearances of Jesus from Jerusalem, and no doubt from Peter during the fifteen days which the two apostles had spent together three years after Paul's conversion. In I Cor. 15 : 1–7 Paul is reproducing the account which the primitive Jerusalem church gave of its own foundation. And in that account Christianity appears, not as an aspiration, not as mere devotion to an ideal of life, not as inculcation of a certain kind of conduct, but as "a piece of information" about something that had actually happened—namely, the atoning death and glorious resurrection of Jesus our Lord.

The Second Epistle to the Corinthians

The First Epistle to the Corinthians did not end all difficulties in the Corinthian church. On the contrary, after the writing of that letter, certain miserable busybodies had sought to draw the Corinthian Christians away from their allegiance to the apostle. A brief visit which Paul had made to Corinth had not ended the trouble. At last Paul had left Ephesus in great distress. He had passed through a terrible personal danger, when he had despaired of life, but more trying still was the thought of Corinth. Finding no relief from his troubles he went to Troas and then across to Macedonia. There at length relief came. Titus, Paul's helper, arrived with good news from Corinth; the church had returned to its allegiance. To give expression to his joy and thanksgiving, Paul wrote the Second Epistle to the Corinthians. In the Epistle he also dealt with the matter of the collection for the poor at Jerusalem, and administered a last rebuke to the Corinthian trouble makers.

In I Corinthians it is the congregation that is in the forefront of interest; in II Corinthians, on the other hand, it is the apostle and his ministry. In this letter, the Apostle Paul lays bare before his readers the very secrets of his heart, and reveals the glories of the ministry which God had intrusted to him. That ministry was the ministry of reconciliation. God and men had been separated by the great gulf of sin, which had brought men under God's wrath and curse. Nothing that men could do could possibly bridge the gulf. But what was impossible with men was possible with God. By the redeeming work of Christ the gulf had been closed; all had been made right again between God and those for whom Christ died.

The Epistle to the Romans

Arriving at Corinth Paul spent three months in that city. During this time he wrote the Epistle to the Romans. Paul was intending to visit the city of Rome. The church at Rome had not been founded by him; it was important, therefore, that in order to prepare for his coming he should set forth plainly to the Romans the gospel which he proclaimed. That is what he does in the Epistle to the Romans. In the Epistle to the Romans, the way of salvation through Christ is set forth more fully than in any other book of the New Testament. In Galatians it is set forth in a polemic way, when Paul was in the midst of a deadly conflict against a religion of works; here it is set forth more calmly and more fully.

In the first great division of the Epistle, Paul sets forth the universal need of salvation. The need is due to sin. All have sinned, and are under God's just wrath and curse. Rom. 1 : 18 to 3 : 20. But the Lord Jesus Christ bore that curse for all believers, by dying for them on the cross; he paid the just penalty of our sins, and clothed us with his perfect righteousness. Ch. 3 : 21–31. This saving work of Christ, and the faith by which it is accepted, were set forth in the Old Testament Scriptures. Ch. 4. The result of the salvation is peace with God, and an assured hope that what God has begun through the gift of Christ, he will bring to a final completion. Ch. 5 : 1–11. Thus, as in Adam all died, by sharing in the guilt of Adam's sin, so in Christ all believers are made alive. Vs. 12–21.

But, Paul goes on, the freedom which is wrought by Christ does not mean freedom to sin; on the contrary it means freedom from the power of sin; it means a new life which is led by the power of God. Ch. 6. What the law could not do, because the power of sin prevented men from keeping its commands, that Christ has accomplished. Ch. 7. Through Christ, believers have been made sons of God; there is to them "no condemnation"; and nothing in this world or the next shall separate them from the love of Christ. Ch. 8.

Toward the spread of this gospel, Paul goes on, the whole course of history has been made to lead. The strange dealings of God both with Jews and Gentiles are part of one holy and mysterious plan. Chs. 9 to 11.

In the last section of the Epistle, Paul shows how the glorious gospel which he has set forth results in holy living from day to day. Chs. 12 to 16.

QUESTIONS ON LESSON XXI

1. What was the occasion for the writing of I Corinthians? of II Corinthians? of Romans?
2. Give outlines of these three Epistles.

LESSON XXII

The First Imprisonment of Paul

After the three months which Paul spent at Corinth on the third missionary journey, he went up to Jerusalem in order to help bear the gifts which he had collected in the Gentile churches for the poor of the Jerusalem church. He was accompanied by a number of helpers, among them Luke, the writer of the Third Gospel and the book of The Acts. Luke had remained behind at Philippi on the second missionary journey, and now, several years later, he joined the apostle again. The portions of the journey where Luke was actually present are narrated in The Acts in great detail and with remarkable vividness.

When Paul came to Miletus on the coast of Asia Minor, he sent to Ephesus for the elders of the Ephesian church, and when they came he held a notable farewell discourse. There was a touching scene when he finally parted from those who loved him so well.

Acts 21:15 to 28:31

Despite prophecies of the imprisonment that awaited him Paul went bravely on to Jerusalem. There he was warmly received by James the brother of the Lord and by the church. Acts 21 : 15–26. But the non-Christian Jews falsely accused him of bringing Gentiles with him into the Temple. Vs. 27–40. There was an onslaught against him, and he was rescued by the Roman chief captain, who took him into the Castle of Antonia which the Romans used to guard the Temple area. On the steps of the castle he was allowed to address the people, ch. 22 : 1–22, who listened to him at first because he used the Aramaic language instead of Greek, but broke out against him again when he spoke of his mission to the Gentiles.

An appeal to his Roman citizenship saved Paul from scourging, Acts 22 : 23–29; and a hearing the next day before the sanhedrin, ch. 22 : 30 to 23 : 10, brought only a quarrel between the Sadducees and the Pharisees. That night Paul had a comforting vision of Christ. V. 11.

A plot of the Jews to waylay Paul and kill him was frustrated by Paul's sister's son, who told the chief captain. The chief captain sent the prisoner with an escort down to Cæsarea where the procurator Felix had his residence. Acts 23 : 12–35. Hearings before Felix brought no decisive result, ch. 24, and Paul was left in prison at Cæsarea for two years until Festus arrived as successor of Felix. Then, in order to prevent being taken to Jerusalem for trial, Paul exercised his right as a Roman citizen by appealing to the court of the emperor. Ch. 25 : 1–12. Accordingly, after a hearing before Herod Agrippa II, who had been made king of a realm northeast of Palestine by the Romans, v. 13; ch. 26 : 32, Paul was sent as a prisoner to Rome, chs. 27 : 1 to 28 : 16.

On the journey he was accompanied by Luke, who has given a detailed account of the voyage—an account which is not only perhaps the chief source of information about the seafaring of antiquity, but also affords a wonderful picture of the way Paul acted in a time of peril. The ship was wrecked on the island of Malta, and it was not until the following spring that the prisoner was brought to Rome. There he remained in prison for two years, chained to a soldier guard, but permitted to dwell in his own hired house and to receive visits from his friends. Acts 28 : 16–31.

During this first Roman imprisonment Paul wrote four of his Epistles—to the Colossians and to Philemon, to the Ephesians, and to the Philippians. Colossians, Philemon, and Ephesians were all written at the same time. Colossians and Ephesians were both sent by the same messenger, Tychicus, and this messenger was accompanied by Onesimus, who bore the Epistle to Philemon.

The Epistle to Philemon

Onesimus was a slave who had run away from Philemon, his master. He had then been converted by Paul, and Paul was now sending him back to his master. The little letter which the apostle wrote on this occasion gives a wonderful picture of the way in which ordinary social relationships like that of master and servant may be made the means of expression for Christian love. Very beautiful also was the relation between Philemon and the apostle through whom he had been converted.

The Epistle to the Colossians

The church at Colossæ, to which the Epistle to the Colossians is addressed, had been founded not by Paul but by one of his helpers, Epaphras. A certain type of false teaching had been brought into the church by those who laid stress upon angels in a way that was harmful to the exclusive position of Christ. In reply, Paul sets forth in the Epistle the majesty of Jesus, who existed from all eternity and was the instrument of God the Father in the creation of the world. This was no new teaching; it is always presupposed in the earlier Epistles of Paul, and about it there was no debate. But in the Epistle to the Colossians, in view of the error that was creeping in through false speculation, Paul took occasion to set forth fully what in the former letters he had presupposed.

The Epistle to the Ephesians

The Epistle to the Ephesians is probably a circular letter addressed to a group of churches of which Ephesus was the center. In this letter the personal element is less prominent than in the other Pauline Epistles; Paul allows his mind to roam freely over the grand reaches of the divine economy. The Church is here especially in view. She is represented as the bride of Christ, and as the culmination of an eternal and gracious plan of God.

The Epistle to the Philippians

The Epistle to the Philippians was probably written later than the other Epistles of the first captivity. The immediate occasion for the writing of the letter was the arrival of a gift from the Philippian church, on account of which Paul desires to express his joy. Paul had always stood in a peculiarly cordial relation to his Philippian converts; he had been willing, therefore, to receive gifts from them, although in other churches he had preferred to make himself independent by laboring at his trade. But the letter is not concerned only or even chiefly with the gifts of the Philippian church. Paul desired also to inform his Philippian brethren about the situation at Rome. His trial is approaching; whether it results in his death or in his release, he is content. But as a matter of fact he expects to see the Philippians again.

Moreover, Paul holds up in the letter the example of Christ, which was manifested in the great act of loving condescension by which he came into the world and endured for our sakes the accursed death on the cross. That humiliation of Christ, Paul says, was followed by exaltation; God has now given to Jesus the name that is above every name.

At the conclusion of the two years in prison in Rome, Paul was released, probably in A.D. 63. This fact is attested not by the book of The Acts, of which the narrative closes at the end of the two years at Rome, but by the Pastoral Epistles of Paul and also by an Epistle of Clement of Rome which was written at about A.D. 95. Clement says that Paul went to Spain. This he probably did immediately after his release. He then went to the East again, for it was in the East that I Timothy and Titus were written.

QUESTIONS ON LESSON XXII

1. Outline the events in the life of Paul which occurred between the departure from Corinth and the end of the first Roman imprisonment.
2. What was the occasion for the writing of Colossians? of Philemon? of Ephesians? of Philippians?
3. Give outlines of these Epistles.

LESSON XXIII
The Close of the Apostolic Age

The Pastoral Epistles

It was observed in the last lesson that Paul was released from his first Roman imprisonment, and went then to Spain and then to the East. At the time when I Timothy was written he has just left Timothy behind at Ephesus when he himself has gone into Macedonia, and now writes the letter with instructions for Timothy as to the way of conducting the affairs of the church. Similarly, the Epistle to Titus was written to guide Titus in his work on the island of Crete.

After this last period of activity in the East, Paul was imprisoned again at Rome. During this second Roman imprisonment he wrote II Timothy, to encourage Timothy and instruct him, and to give to him and to the Church a farewell message just before his own death, which he was expecting very soon.

The two Epistles to Timothy and the Epistle to Titus, which are called the Pastoral Epistles, are similar to one another in important respects. They all lay stress upon soundness of teaching and upon the organization of the Church. In the closing years of his life Paul provided for the permanence of his work; the period of origination was over and the period of conservation had begun. It was not God's will that every Christian generation should have revealed to it anew the whole of the gospel. What is true in one age is true in all ages. It was a salutary thing, therefore, that the Pastoral Epistles provided for the preservation of the faith which was once for all delivered unto the saints.

Soon after the writing of II Timothy, Paul was beheaded at Rome. This event, which is attested in altogether credible Christian tradition outside of the New Testament, took place within the reign of the Emperor Nero—that is, before A.D. 68.   At the time of the great fire at Rome in A.D. 64 Nero had persecuted the Christians, as is narrated by Tacitus, the Roman historian.   But at that time Paul probably escaped by being out of the city; his execution probably did not occur until several years later.

At about the time of the death of Paul disastrous events were taking place in Palestine.   James the brother of the Lord had been put to death by the Jews in A.D. 62, according to Josephus the Jewish historian, or a few years later according to another account.   In A.D. 66 the Jews rose in revolt against the Romans.   In the war that followed there was a terrible siege of Jerusalem.   Before the siege the Christians in the city had fled to Pella, east of the Jordan.   Jerusalem was captured by the Romans in A.D. 70, and the Temple destroyed.

From that time on, the Church in Palestine ceased to be of great relative importance; the gospel had passed for the most part to the Gentiles.   A number of the apostles remained for many years, however, to guide and instruct the Church, and important books of the New Testament were written in this period either by the apostles themselves or by those who stood under their direction.

The Epistle to the Hebrews

Even before the destruction of the Temple, the original disciples had begun to labor far and wide among the Gentiles.   It was perhaps during this early period that the Epistle to the Hebrews was written. The name of the author is unknown, but the book is truly apostolic

—that is, it was written either by an apostle or by one who wrote under the direction of the apostles. The Epistle is intended to celebrate the all-sufficiency of Christ as the great High Priest, who has made atonement by his own blood, as distinguished from the Old Testament types that were intended to point forward to him.

The First Epistle of Peter

Some years before the destruction of Jerusalem, the apostle Peter left Palestine. In the course of his missionary journeys he went to Rome, and it was perhaps from Rome that he wrote the First Epistle of Peter, the word "Babylon" in I Peter 5 : 13 being perhaps a figurative designation of Rome as the "Babylon" of that age. The Epistle was addressed to Christians in Asia Minor, and was intended to encourage the readers to Christian fortitude in the midst of persecution. The gospel proclaimed in the Epistle is the one great apostolic gospel of Christ's redeeming work which was also proclaimed by Paul.

The Second Epistle of Peter ; The Epistle of Jude

The Second Epistle of Peter was written by the apostle to warn his readers against false teaching and urge them to be faithful to the authority of the apostles and of the Scriptures. Closely related to II Peter is the Epistle of Jude, which was written by one of the brothers of Jesus. The apostle Peter, in accordance with a thoroughly credible Christian tradition, finally suffered a martyr's death at Rome.

The apostle John, the son of Zebedee, became the head of the Church in Asia Minor, where, at Ephesus, he lived until nearly the end of the first century. During this period he wrote five books of the New Testament.

The Gospel According to John was written to supplement the other three Gospels which had long been in use. It contains much of the most precious and most profound teaching of our Lord, as it had been stored up in the memory of the "beloved disciple"; and it presents the glory of the Word of God as that glory had appeared on earth to an eyewitness.

The Epistles of John

The First Epistle of John was written in order to combat certain errors which were creeping into the Church in Asia Minor and in order to present to the readers the true Christian life of love, founded upon the Son of God who had come in the flesh, and begun by the new birth which makes a man a child of God.

The Second Epistle of John is a very brief letter written to warn an individual church of the same kind of error as is combated in I John.

The Third Epistle is addressed to an individual Christian named Gaius, who is praised for his hospitality to visiting missionaries, which was the more praiseworthy because it was in contrast to the inhospitality of a certain Diotrephes. The little letter sheds a flood of light upon the details of congregational life in the last period of the Apostolic Age.

The Book of Revelation

The book of Revelation is based upon a revelation which the apostle John had received during a banishment to the island of Patmos, off the coast of Asia Minor, not far from Ephesus. Probably the book itself was written on the same island. The book contains letters to seven churches of western Asia Minor which are intended to encourage or warn them in accordance with the needs of every individual congregation. The whole book is a tremendous prophecy, which strengthens the faith of the Church in the midst of persecutions and trials by revealing the plan of God, especially as it concerns the second coming of our Lord and the end of the world. Details of future events, especially times and seasons, are not intended to be revealed, but rather great principles both of good and of evil, which manifest themselves in various ways in the subsequent history of the Church. The prophecy, however, will receive its highest and final fulfillment only when our Lord shall come again, and bring in the final reign of righteousness and the blessedness of those whom he has redeemed.

QUESTIONS ON LESSON XXIII

1. When, where, and why were the three Pastoral Epistles written?
2. Outline the life of Paul after his release from the first Roman imprisonment.
3. What is known about the latter part of the life of Peter?
4. What was the occasion for the writing of I Peter? of II Peter? of Jude? What are the characteristics of these letters?
5. What is known about the latter part of the life of John?
6. What were the date and the purpose of the Gospel According to John; of the Epistles of John; of the book of Revelation.

Other Related Titles by Solid Ground

In addition to *The Glorious History of Redemption,* we are delighted to offer several titles connected with Old Princeton.

Notes on Galatians by Machen is a reprint that is long overdue, in light of the present-day battle of the doctrine articulated in Galatians.

The Origin of Paul's Religion by Machen penetrates to the heart of the matter and speaks to many of the contemporary attacks upon the purity of the Gospel of Christ.

Biblical and Theological Studies by the professors of Princeton in 1912, at the centenary celebration of the Seminary. Articles are by men like Allis, Vos, Warfield, Machen, Wilson and others.

Theology on Fire: Vols. 1 & 2 by J.A. Alexander is the two volumes of sermons by this brilliant scholar from Princeton Seminary.

A Shepherd's Heart by J.W. Alexander is a volume of outstanding expository sermons from the pastoral ministry of one of the leading preachers of the 19th century.

Evangelical Truth by Archibald Alexander is a volume of practical sermons intended to be used for Family Worship.

The Lord of Glory by B.B. Warfield is one of the best treatments of the doctrine of the Deity of Christ ever written. It is a true classic.

The Power of God unto Salvation by Warfield is the first book of sermons published by this master-theologian.

The Person & Work of the Holy Spirit by Warfield is a compilation of all the sermons, articles and book reviews by a master-theologian on a theme that should interest every child of God. Brilliant in every way!

Grace & Glory by Geerhardus Vos is a series of addresses delivered in the chapel to the students at Princeton. John Murray said of him, "Dr. Vos is, in my judgment, the most penetrating exegete it has been my privilege to know, and I believe, the most incisive exegete that has appeared in the English-speaking world in this century."

Princeton Sermons: *Chapel Addresses from 1891-92* by B.B. Warfield, W.H. Green, C.W. Hodge, John D. Davis and More. According to Joel Beeke, this is "a treasure-trove of practical Christianity delivered by some of the greatest preachers and seminary teachers America has ever known."

Call us at **1-205-443-0311**
Send us an e-mail at **mike.sgcb@gmail.com**
Visit us on line at **www.solid-ground-books.com**

CPSIA information can be obtained
at www.ICGtesting.com
Printed in the USA
JSHW030856220121
11081JS00005B/166